THE PRACTICE OF PLANNING

Other Books by David W. Ewing

Long-Range Planning for Management (*Editor*)

Effective Marketing Action (*Editor*)

Incentives for Executives (*Coeditor*)

The Managerial Mind

The Practice of Planning

by David W. Ewing

Associate Editor
Harvard Business Review

HARPER & ROW, PUBLISHERS

NEW YORK, EVANSTON, AND LONDON

1817

Contents

Preface

A few years ago I accepted an invitation to talk about planning to a group of businessmen in a midwestern city. In preparing the talk I began putting together many notes I had collected on concepts and methods of planning, but the more I thought about these notes, the more inadequate they seemed to become. They were based on what different authorities *said* about planning, not on what organizations actually *did* when they went about the work of formulating and implementing plans. Between the words and the acts there was, it seemed to me, a large gap. Moreover, many of the questions the authorities were not writing about were, I knew, topics of vital concern to managers in business, governmental, and educational organizations.

Discarding my original notes, I began studying cases and records of planners in action, seeking to deduce from them what some of the "secrets" of planning really were. A few of the ideas stressed in this book were born during that investigation. Many of the men at the meeting I addressed encouraged me with the start I had made, so afterward I kept working on the approach, talking to people who were actually engaged in planning and examining as many case examples as I could find.

The result is this text. It is largely interpretative, and sometimes speculative; yet it deals, I believe, with questions of almost universal importance to executives in business, government, and education and to students in these fields:

1. How does management choose goals that are right for its organization?

2. What techniques of formal and informal analysis will help the organization formulate programs for achieving the goals?

Many people have helped me in the work on this book. Richard McAdoo of Harper & Row has offered constructive suggestions at all stages. Magazines like *Forbes, Business Week, Fortune, The Business Quarterly,* and others cited in the text have been a generous source of help. A number of business executives have taken time to comment candidly on the problems and opportunities of planning. Mrs. Alice McDowell typed the first draft of the manuscript, and I am grateful to Miss Vicki Boggs for finishing up numerous revisions and taking care of a great deal of correspondence. As with former books, my wife took on many added responsibilities in order to make it possible for me to work on the manuscript.

It must be emphasized that the views set forth in this book are my own and do not necessarily represent the thinking of other members of the Harvard Business School Faculty or the *Harvard Business Review* staff.

DAVID W. EWING

THE PRACTICE OF PLANNING

Planning's Role in Perspective

1

The modern corporation is one of history's great surprises. Born an artificial person in the obscurity of nineteenth-century state statutes, it was never seen as a giant of the future. It is rarely glorified and almost never obtains more than a small place in American schoolbooks; its births and deaths usually go unnoticed in the newspapers; it is not commemorated by statues or plaques in front of public buildings. Yet it accounts for much of the rise of the United States and other nations in the West. Its impact on domestic, cultural, and public life is exceeded only by its impact on economic development. In the United States, government is making increasing use of the private corporation in order to achieve national goals in space, military defense, and international relations. In the East, several Communist nations, while entertaining no ambitions to become capitalist, are experimenting more and more boldly with economic organizations possessing certain properties and characteristics of the Western corporation.

Although the leaders of corporations have long been branded as conservative in a political sense, their record has been anything but conservative in other respects. They have brought on radical changes in the quality and character of American life. Mass production, mass distribution, modern food processing, electronic data processing, television, rapid transportation, home appliances—these and other corporation-led revolutions have altered our daily lives more broadly, more profoundly, than any series of innovations in law, medicine, or the arts. What is perhaps most striking of all is that no letup of this revolutionary zeal is in sight. Having solved problems of food, clothing, suburban housing, heating, private transportation, and a host of other economic matters, the corporation is now turning to tasks once considered the preserve of government. Its current experiments with new approaches to urban renewal, teaching aids in public education, retraining of the unemployed, programs for "systems management" of water resources and waste disposal, food for underdeveloped nations overseas, and other needs—these ventures have shown remarkable potential. Increasing numbers of corporate leaders find themselves stirred by the vision of George Champion, board chairman of The Chase Manhattan Bank, who said in 1966: "Just imagine what could be accomplished if some of our competitive zest were channeled into public service. Think of the good that could be done if business were to launch an all-out campaign of creative competition with government in developing imaginative new approaches to economic and social problems."

What combination of resources and abilities accounts for the modern corporation's ability to innovate and prosper?

First, the corporation must have managers and employees with vitality. It must have managers who like to use their brains, specialists who want to innovate, energetic employees who seek to achieve. The company itself may nurture the talents, ambitions, and energies of its people and so combine them as to produce a synergistic effect; but the qualities must be there to begin with or the organization can never become more than a legal shell. It is no accident that companies are devoting more and more money and time to man-power training, development, and motivation.

Second, the corporation must have a social, cultural, and political environment conducive to its mode of operation. It depends urgently and immediately on many things which, in Western countries, are now often taken for granted: in people, such simple qualities as honesty, a sense of fair play, confidence, a propensity to save; in institutions, such qualities as respect for the individual and an insistence on law and order. For these qualities, the corporation must look first to the family, the church, the school system, civic organizations. Again, it can reinforce and strengthen the qualities, but unless they are cultivated first by others it has nothing to work with. In this sense, the commercial corporation has a symbiotic relationship with noncommercial groups.

But, of course, vitality and a conducive environment are not by themselves enough. The corporation needs a *third* resource: plant and equipment, power supplies, land, money. Fortunately, all of these are in relative abundance in the United States (and in many other nations of the West). For this abundance the corporation owes part of its thanks to many agencies who are resource producers; for instance, banks, equipment builders, private inventors, realtors. A number of these agencies have themselves benefited from the personal vitality mentioned earlier; hence they have sought vigorously to improve their offerings and have taught user corporations to be healthily discontented with the status quo. They have, in effect, injected some of their own vitality into the main stream of corporate life.

Fourth, there must be markets. It is true that markets do not spring up spontaneously; usually life is breathed into them by the very businesses that depend on them. Nevertheless, there must be the makings of markets, the potentials. There must be people, agencies, civic groups, social organizations, and governments who have purchasing power, who can be made interested in using corporate goods and services, and who are so distributed that the goods can be brought to them economically. These conditions have not existed in all civilizations and cultures.

Although the four resources described combine to form a potent base, they still are far from enough to explain corporate success. Which people will do what jobs? Who will decide what to do? Who is responsible for the methods chosen to carry out tasks? When conflicts arise between individuals and groups, who will arbitrate them? Obviously, there is a need for organization in the structural and procedural sense. This is the *fifth* requirement. Organization does not necessarily mean organization charts; rather, it implies a more basic understanding of decision centers and the relationships between them. Of the hundreds of technical accomplishments of business leaders in the United States, the art of effective organization ranks among the most significant.

Alfred Sloan of General Motors Corporation is usually singled out as the genius in this field, although the extent of his contribution to the nation's economic might has yet to be popularly appreciated. But there are many others—thousands of them—who account for our present-day knowledge of organization. Sears Roebuck has experimented successfully with so-called "flat" organization structures having a minimum of pyramidal layers of authority. DuPont has contributed the concept of top management by committee; with Minnesota Mining and Manufacturing Company, it is also the coauthor of independent divisions for the development of new products (so that the entrepreneurial spirit will not be lost in the operations myopia of the manufacturing divisions). The joint venture has been pushed to new variations and forms by small and large companies. Businessmen have also been advancing the art of what has been called "symbiotic marketing," that is, the alliance of two or more firms' resources and programs so that the marketing potential of each is improved. Pushing the frontiers of know-how farther still, a midwest plant is working on a way of running complex production operations without the presence of supervisors. One could go on at great length with similar examples. In terms of getting work done by people, they have at least as much significance as has the arrangement of component parts in increasing machine efficiency.

However, even if a firm had exceptional strength in all the foregoing respects, it still would not be able to perform like the modern corporation unless it could meet other conditions. A *sixth* requirement is a kind of discipline. There must be some measure of conformity so that employees know what to expect of one another. Their abilities to innovate and create must be channeled, else there can be little effective innovation at all. The means to this end is a set of policies. For example, a policy that the customer is always right makes it possible for employees in retailing to work swiftly and consistently and without wasting endless hours going over old arguments about how to treat customers; a policy that inventories shall be kept at high enough levels to minimize the risk of running out of stock makes it possible to go a step farther and work out efficient ordering and re-ordering rules; if a corporation has a policy that it will not seek to be "Number One" in its industry in research but an alert follower of the research leader, the men and women who direct tests in the laboratory and those who hire scientists and engineers can find ways to proceed so their work will dovetail with the expectations of marketing and investment managers. (Just the opposite policies would, of course, be equally advantageous for this purpose.)

But how will the executives of diversified and often far-flung operations know whether or not their policies are being followed? How are they to evaluate and compare the work of individuals and departments? If a division or project is falling below the standards of efficiency and earnings performance set for it, how will management learn of this before it is too late to correct matters? Clearly, the modern corporation must meet a *seventh* requirement: a system of effective control. There is probably no leading company in North America or western Europe today that could be where it is without techniques of management and operations control. Sometimes these are qualitative: simple reports and verifications. More often they are quantitative: figures on costs, sales volume, price, assets, employee turnover, and so forth. In operations, concepts like statistical quality control have been extremely significant tools, enabling managers not only to keep better apprised of trends in performance but also to free themselves for other executive tasks. Automatic data processing, of course, is the widely heralded new tool for operations control; there is no telling how many companies would be far off their present pace without it. In administration there are procedures like budgeting and "management by exception." Progress with them has been so fast and far-reaching that methods which were well accepted only forty years ago would seem crude and naïve to the business school student of today.

But we still do not have the combination that explains the efficacy of the modern corporation. The seven factors described help us considerably, but something vital is missing. It is as if we were trying to open a combination lock requiring eight turns, and we had made the first seven stops correctly but were trying to shake the lock open without turning to the last number. In which direction should the corporation move? What goals should it seek? How shall it decide on its goals?

Unless it finds its own answers to these questions, the corporation will have to respond to commands from elsewhere in society—government, perhaps, or labor unions. It will forever be what the psychologists call "other-directed" instead of "inner-directed." It will never be able to hew paths, but only to follow the beaten ones; and beaten paths, as Eric Johnson once said, are for beaten men.

The *eighth* capability, the one yet to be described, is what is called planning. Planning is one of the newer concepts of management—new, at least, as compared to approaches like control, organization, policy, and financial management. It is, as we shall see in later chapters, a concept about which there is much ferment and variety of opinion. Planning is far more important to the modern corporation than it was to corporate ancestors of the early twentieth century and nineteenth century. This is because new technologies, proliferating public needs, product diversification, accelerating social change, and other trends put an enormous premium on the ability of management to select skillfully from among many possible goals, to make its selection at an opportune time, and to channel the organization's efforts swiftly in the desired direction. Indeed, to understand planning is to understand a process which, as much as or more than any other resource or capability, gives the modern corporation its unique ability to prosper in a world of continuing change.

Guidelines

2

When we want to build a new house or a new machine tool, we often begin by laying out the ideal specifications of the thing to be built, without reference to what we think at the moment we are able or can afford to create. If there were no limitations of cost, materials, or ingenuity, what would we like to see made? We think of the question almost wholly in terms of our needs, problems, aspirations. Then, with our ideal specifications in hand, we commence to work back and see what it is practical to try to accomplish. We begin compromising, seeking to get as near the ideal as possible within the realm of what is feasible.

It is useful to begin thinking of planning in much the same way. What, ideally, would we like the planning process to accomplish? With this question answered, we can turn to our own organizations, be they in business, education, government, community service, or the military, and examine the question of how close to the ideal our planning can reasonably come.

Failure to begin in this manner may well account for some of the agonies with planning experienced thus far. It may account for part of the confusion over the matter of what planning is and what it should do. It may also account for the lack of rapport between theorists and "experts," on the one hand, and managers and practitioners, on the other. This lack of rapport is hard to overlook. In too many organizations today from Capitol Hill to Knob Hill we find the spectacle of bright, dedicated, highly proficient staff planners working on one floor, sending reports to and sometimes talking with operating executives on another floor, *but not influencing them very often.* There are various possible explanations for this; but one good reason, I believe, is a lack of common understanding about what planning is and should be.

In this chapter let us first examine some requirements and specifications for planning as executives would ideally have it (with some additional notes on what they should not try to have planning do). Then we can set forth a definition of planning activity.

Outline of the Ideal

What would the ideal planning process or plan accomplish? It would do at least seven things:

1. *It would lead to a better position or standing for the organization.*

Planning would not be an end in itself; it would be a means to an end. It would be rated no better than the profit, volume, prestige, efficiency, and/or other results it helps management achieve. Many good planners insist that it is not enough to say simply that planning should lead to improvement; they stipulate improvement *in relation to the opportunities available.* If a company with profit goals is riding a market wave, it may be able to improve its earnings just by continuing to operate. That would not be enough from a planning viewpoint. The requirement is satisfied only if planning enables the company to take greater advantage of the market wave than it otherwise could, thereby increasing its profit position by more than it would have without plans and programs.

2. *It would help the organization progress in the ways that its management considers most suitable.*

For instance, if management is more interested in stability and moderate profits than in the highest possible profits at the risk of instability, planning can help accomplish the former; or, if a government aid agency is less interested in quick-acting, high-cost crash programs of aid than in highly efficient slower programs, planning can help accomplish the latter.

In their book *Business Policy: Text and Cases,* Edmund P. Learned, C. Roland Christensen, Kenneth R. Andrews, and William D. Guth refer to two interesting examples that can be used to illustrate this point.[1] They note that a certain food company purposely courts disaster with production slowdowns and erratic commodity prices in order to maximize the company's chances of earning a high profit. "But the choice is made knowingly and the return, if success is achieved, is likely to be correspondingly great. Temperamentally the president is willing to live under this pressure and presumably has recourse if disaster strikes." For contrast the authors refer to an office equipment company that is managed with modest top-management aspirations for growth (so much so that the junior executives are unhappy). In these two situations planning would be very different.

3. *It would help every manager think, decide, and act more effectively for progress in the desired direction.*

Ideally, planning should help managers and supervisors solve ordinary problems quickly, "on the spot," and on their own authority—and refer unusual problems more quickly and intelligently to the right senior executives or committees. For instance, if a department head is debating whether or not to expand a warehouse or build a brand new one, his knowledge of corporate plans should help him make that decision. It would help him know the answers to such questions as: Is the business in question due to

[1] Homewood, Ill.: Richard D. Irwin, 1965, p. 27.

be expanded? Or is it going to be "phased out" after a while? Will investments be made in new types of distribution facilities that will take over some of the conventional functions of warehouse space? Or, if a manager is considering different ways of self-development through training and reading, his familiarity with organizational goals and programs should help him choose his course wisely. For instance, will the organization soon be making a major effort to add branches and services overseas, in which case important new opportunities for employees will be created? Will new programs necessitate more emphasis in decision making on quantitative tools, in which case there are learning opportunities in that area?

It is sometimes said in moments of infatuation with planning that it spells the difference between corporate success and failure, or that a good plan is the key to corporate survival. This is nonsense. No plan ever made an organization successful. No plan ever spelled the difference between success and failure. Only managerial *decisions* can do that. If a plan helps with the making of decisions, then and only then does it affect results.

The chief executive of a growing business concern was asked if he had a formal planning program. His answer:

If you are asking me, "Do you do a lot of planning?" my answer is "Yes." If you are asking me whether we print a number of papers about it, headed "Planning," the answer is "No."

I am engaged in planning, 12 hours a day, every day. I don't know how you could run a business without thinking of the three- to five-year implications of everything you do today.[2]

For him, planning counts for nothing unless it is tied in with what his management group is doing and the way it does it. Such an executive is understandably prejudiced against planning as it is so often offered—as an analytical exercise rather than a decision-making tool. Help us act wisely! Help us decide correctly! That is what the operating executive asks of planners and plans.

[2] Stewart Thompson, *How Companies Plan* (New York: American Management Association, 1962), p. 49.

"Effective corporate planning," writes Myles Mace, a former vice-president of Litton Industries, Inc., and now active as a corporate director and Harvard Business School professor, "does not consist simply of a system. Rather, it is an administrative process and a critically important job which should concern the management of every concern."[3] Robert H. Schaffer refers to this statement to bolster his criticism of planners who go overboard for method and concept:

For the corporate planner to focus chiefly on the technical tasks related to the construction of "plans" is to fly in the face of Mace's assertion. It is to make the false assumption that planning can indeed exist as an isolatable function of management.

This is perhaps the single most illusory and dangerous management fable of our times. This fable permits corporate planners to view with disdain many of the tough realities of corporate life or see them as obstacles or barriers to the performance of the planner's sophisticated work when, in fact, these so-called blocks or obstacles should be the very guts of their jobs.[4]

4. *It would help keep the organization flexible.*

Ideally, planning should exert a very positive thrust on the organization, without being too rigid. "It is possible to conceive of strategy as being firm and influential without its being cast in concrete."[5] The ideal planning activity makes managers prepared, yet not overprepared. It does not make them musclebound, as some athletes become, or information-bound as students when they memorize too much data. The aim of planning should be to make managers faster on their feet, more imaginative, more inquiring, but not slaves of a master scheme in a desk drawer.

5. *It would stimulate a cooperative, integrated, enthusiastic approach to organizational problems.*

[3] "The President and Corporate Planning," *Harvard Business Review*, January–February, 1965, p. 49.
[4] From "Strategy for the Corporate Planning Function," *Business Management*, July, 1967.
[5] Edmund P. Learned *et al.*, *op. cit.*, p. 24.

As L. Eugene Root, a vice-president of Lockheed Aircraft Corporation, and George Steiner, a professor at University of California (Los Angeles), have noted, there is a natural tendency in most operating organizations to concentrate on immediate problems, isolate them from other problems, and develop piecemeal solutions. A patchwork of conflicting long- and short-run consequences results between different groups and departments.[6]

The ideal planning program would counteract this tendency. It would help to make a manager more understanding of his own and others' roles in fulfilling the corporate mission. It would give him a framework or perspective for viewing the questions and decisions that confront him, so that he could see them not as isolated issues but as parts of a whole.

6. *It would indicate to management how to evaluate and check up on progress toward the planned objectives.*

What kind of feedback is to be sought? What indicators of progress are important to watch? Unless the answers to questions like these are clear, managers will not be able to tell whether they have succeeded in going where they were supposed to go, or how they can go beyond.

Progress measurements in short-term planning are different from measurements in long-term planning. In the former, M. J. Kami (formerly with International Business Machines and Xerox) has noted, actual results are properly compared with planned results. The comparisons can be fiscal—for example, actual monthly revenues and expenditures—as well as physical— such as sales productivity, manufacturing output, personnel hired. But in long-term planning such precision is self-defeating; there are more unknowns, more subjective estimates. As Kami points

6 "The Lockheed Aircraft Corporation Master Plan," in David W. Ewing, editor, *Long-Range Planning for Management* (New York: Harper & Row, 1964), p. 258.

out, there may be no intention, when the long-range plan is formulated, of some day matching results *closely* with objectives.
"It is normal in long-range planning to have a 'planning gap' for
future years—a difference between objectives and presently expected results. Long-range planning is successful when later
plans close the 'planning gap' of earlier plans. The rapidity and
extent to which these 'unknown needs' are converted to 'known
programs' is an important measure of planning efficiency."[7]

7. *It would lead to socially and economically useful results.*

One thing about planning that impresses many executives is
that it adds to their ability to *elect* the kinds of things their organizations can do and ways of doing them. Living wholly in the
present, management can only react and respond to events; notions about business philosophy, morality, and public service
tend to get shelved because they seem irrelevant and "academic."

The ideal planning process "brings out the best" in the organization and helps it represent the business, educational, political,
or military system (as the case may be) to the public as well as
it can.

What Planning Is Not

Now let us look at the other side of the planning coin. What
should we *not* expect planning to do?

First, planning is not words, communication, and public relations. Such vehicles may be useful in planning or by-products
of it, but by no means should they be equated with it. Here is a
revealing passage from a group report of business executives at-
tending the Advanced Management Program at the Harvard
Business School:

It is a serious error to believe that flowery statements about planning in the annual report are enough. These statements might im-
press stockholders *but may have the deadly consequence of being*

[7] See George A. Steiner, *Managerial Long-Range Planning* (New York: Mc-
Graw-Hill Book Company, 1963), p. 253.

believed by management itself, thus incurring the attendant delusion that someone is, in fact, actually carrying out this function. This is one of a number of ways of carrying out lip service. Informal conversations with a number of members of the 46th Advanced Management Program, while certainly not yielding conclusive evidence, indicate that paying lip service to the planning-for-change function is more commonplace than was expected. In some instances, top management may really believe that it has an efficient planning function operating when in fact this may not be true at all.[8] [Italics added.]

Second, planning is not the same thing as budgeting. One company I know of impresses this distinction on managers by separating its budget (called the profit plan) from the plan of action. The two are presented at different times of the year so that they will not be confused.

Of course, there is an important—sometimes intimate—relationship between planning and budgeting (see Chapter 7 for a detailed discussion of this point). The budget is a tool of planning. It is, as Walter B. Schaffir, a planning executive at Western Union, has noted, "the essential and inescapable expression of a plan in financial terms." Using these terms, the budget shows what resources are required and what pay-offs are required. Not surprisingly, the same department in the company is sometimes made responsible for both planning and budgeting. But here the similarity ends. A budget does not tell how certain goals will be accomplished. It does not tell what assumptions these goals are predicated on, or what alternatives there are. Nor does it tell anything about the appropriateness of these goals—or of the budget itself, for that matter—to the aims and abilities of the organization. As many executives have stressed, and as Schaffir has pointed out, the kind of man and background that may be excellent for budgeting is not necessarily suitable at all for planning. Planning calls not only for a different perspective on operations but, more important still, for different activities and relationships among those doing the planning.

[8] "A Syndicate Report by the 46th Advanced Management Program: Top Management's Role in Planning and Implementing Change," November, 1964.

Third, planning is not forecasting. Equating the two is probably the oldest trap that managers and teachers in business and public administration have fallen into. While it is true that forecasting may be a part of the planning process, forecasting is by no means all of planning. Some excellent planning has been done with no forecasting to speak of. What is more, some fine plans have been made which have flown in the face of forecasts.

Fourth, planning is not report writing. I remember one marketing manager addressing himself very articulately to the problems which he and other marketing people had in writing plans for their departments. He pointed out how little time there was to write them; yet they must be written. He stressed how little time other executives had to read them; yet it was important that they do so. He went on to talk about how selective marketing plans should be, how long, how readable, how they should be organized. He emphasized everything but the most important thing of all: that the writing out of a program may have little or nothing to do with planning effectiveness! Use of written plans may indeed help in evaluation and coordination, but the documents are useful only insofar as they symbolize actual efforts made.

Fifth, planning is not the maintenance of a "planning department," or the establishment of any other organizational device, although formal departments and appointments may be extremely valuable. An executive making a study of long-range planning in the electronics industry as a Sloan Fellow at Massachusetts Institute of Technology gave me this statement:

The presence or absence of a formal organization is to a large extent unrelated to the amount of serious well-directed future planning activity that takes place. It could very well be the case that the planning in companies with highly organized planning activities may be completely ineffective.

Sixth, planning is not an attempt to avoid risk taking. Peter Drucker's exposition of this point for long-range planning has application to shorter-range planning too:

It is not even an attempt to minimize risk. Indeed, any such attempt can only lead to irrational and unlimited risk and to certain disaster.

The central fact about economic activity is that, by definition, it commits present resources to future and therefore highly uncertain expectations. To take risk is therefore the essence of economic activity. . . . But while it is futile to try to eliminate risk, and questionable to try to minimize it, it is essential that the risks taken be the *right risks*. The end result of successful long-range planning must be a capacity to take greater risk; for this is the only way to improve entrepreneurial performance. To do this, however, we must know and understand the risks we take.[9]

Seventh, planning is not necessarily an attempt to improve operating efficiency. Failure to see that efficiency-consciousness and cost improvement may lead in quite different directions from planning—especially strategic planning—has been a source of great aggravation to leaders in corporate planning. In companies where the cost-efficiency view prevails, states John B. Mc-Kitterick of General Electric Company (which obviously does not belong to that unfortunate group), "planning has tended to become a mere administrative process of endless criteria, and the creative quality of the alternatives examined is scarcely worthy of the sterile perfection of the decision system applied. . . . Yet, as we have seen, the profit rewards from endlessly doing the old things more efficiently also are trivial."[10]

A Definition

In the light of all this—the positive attributes as well as the negative ones—I like to define planning as *a method of guiding managers so that their decisions and actions affect the future of the organization in a consistent and rational manner, and in a*

[9] "Long-Range Planning Means Risk-Taking," in David W. Ewing, *op. cit.*, p. 9; originally printed in *Management Science*, April, 1959.

[10] "The Nature of the Involvement of Marketing Management and Profit Failure," in Charles H. Hindersman, editor, *Marketing Precision and Executive Action* (Chicago: American Marketing Association, 1962), p. 85.

way desired by top management. Such variations as "long-range," "intermediate-range," and "short-range" planning all fall under this definition, differing only in the time span covered (and, by inference, the amount of change desired); so do such variations as "strategic," "tactical," and "operational" planning, which we will turn to in Chapter 3.

In the proposed definition, the words "affect the future" are obviously key words. "We think the future can be *made* better," Sam Kalow, product manager of International Business Machine's dictating machine operation, once said. This is the spirit with which many aggressive managers in business, education, and government have approached planning—and the spirit which our definition is intended to catch. Peter Drucker's phrase for it is "the futurity of present decisions." He reminds us how often the decisions executives make today, whether or not under the penumbra of planning, carry with them assumptions about the future, long-range as well as short-range. For instance, a decision to build a steel plant in 1959, when there was nothing but the technology of that time available, meant in effect that management was betting the old technology would be useful at least for another fifteen or twenty years, for the possibilities of modifying the plant would be so limited that a whole new investment would be required to apply a major change in steel technology.

The word "consistent" in the definition is also vital. As executives in almost every field of work see planning, one of its greatest potential values is in helping coordinate the work that goes on. Take the recent history of urban renewal. Officials of an urban renewal program will, let us say, acquire a tract of land for redevelopment. This will take several years of hard, painstaking work with city officials, business interests, political factions, and other groups. Then, with the land finally marked for renewal—the first great stage of the program triumphant—what happens? The highway administration comes along and pre-empts part of the tract for a large cloverleaf intersection! Such lack of coordination, going on as it does in not one but many areas of government endeavor, makes a strong case for a kind of economic planning at the federal and state levels: not ambitious in-depth planning of the sort that socialist governments use, but simply enough planning to avoid needless undermining of one agency's efforts by another.

The word "rational" is important, too. Planning works through operating managers who are under great pressures most of the time and are liable to be distracted at any moment of a typical day by news of a crisis somewhere in their departments. They do not have the luxury that some professional men enjoy—uninterrupted hours for thinking through a problem. Planning should, therefore, help the executive to counteract distraction, interruption, and operating crises when considering matters with important future implications.

George L. Chamberlain, a consultant for General Electric Company, once said that he could not look at a department plan and, on the face of it, evaluate its workability. But he added: "I could say if it is incomplete, if the manager has forgotten to make provision for doing something he wanted to do. The manager ought to provide some means of bringing about every result he plans to achieve. A plan shouldn't be just wishful thinking."[11]

Of especially great significance are the words "desired by top management." This is the phrase that implies goal setting; it implies a conscious management effort to look at itself and its environment and, on the basis of facts and aspirations, make the best choice possible in the range of alternatives. Such strategic choices will be the focus of much attention later in this book.

In football, a key step in the game is taken before the first whistle is ever blown. It comes when the coaches review the game films of the coming opponent and the condition of their own team and talk with the players about strategy for the forthcoming contest. What kind of game should they expect? How should they try to play it? Will it be a contest on the lines, with

11 Stewart Thompson, *op. cit.*, p. 73.

one trying to wear down the other in the hope of opening up scoring in the fourth quarter? Will it be a wide-open, high-scoring game from the start, with the possibility of its being won early on some "long bombs"? Are the opponent's conventional defenses to be expected, or something new in the way of blitzing the passer or position-jumping? The success with which coaches and players answer these questions has no small part to play in how the team performs during the game.

Similarly, in planning it is helpful to know what kind of action to expect when the work gets under way. If it is seen as a tool of decision making which is to be used in doing the same kinds of things managers have always done, only in the hope of doing them a little better, it will be taken up with realistic expectations, and confidence in using it should grow with advancing use. But if it is seen as some kind of elite function which has a princely existence all its own, disillusionment will almost surely follow.

Goals and Stages

3

The first major stage in planning has to do with setting organizational goals: strategic planning. The second stage is concerned with the execution of programs for reaching the goals. Success in the second stage is related to what is done in the first: the goals selected must be feasible for the organization and calculated to inspire enthusiasm, else the execution is likely to fail no matter how much hard work goes into it. Although both stages will be analyzed in this book, most of our attention will be devoted to strategic planning.

Goals and Strategies

To gain an overview of strategic planning, let us consider briefly the kinds of procedure used, ways of expressing goals, and some characteristics of strategic plans.

General Procedures

Who establishes corporate goals? In one good-sized company I know, a committee of top executives draws up every year or so

21

a statement of what they think the corporate goals should be, including objectives for the main divisions and departments of the company. Copies of this statement are circulated to the division and departmental managers. After the managers have gone over the statements, they meet with members of the top executive committee to discuss the objectives. The objectives may be revised upward or downward in this discussion; they may be revised in character; or they may be left untouched. In any event, not until there has been a meeting of the minds on these matters does the executive committee instruct the operating managers to draw up programs and budgets showing how the goals can be accomplished.

In divisionalized companies, the strategic side of planning is likely to follow such a general pattern, differing only in detail from what has been described. It should be noted, though, that sometimes the first "go-around" with the operating managers is but the beginning. When a set of tentatively agreed-on division strategies has been assembled, it may be a major task to make them mesh together and convert them into an over-all capital or financial plan. Typically there is a great deal of give-and-take, back-and-forth negotiation and compromise between managers—behind the scenes, of course, and informally conducted.

In smaller organizations, an over-all goal is likely to be conceived by the chief executive and talked over with his top sales, production, engineering, and other managers. Because of the closeness of the managerial group in a smaller firm, goals are often understood with far greater clarity than is possible in the administrative echelons of large corporations.

Donald J. Smalter of International Minerals and Chemical Corporation is well known among industrial planners for his presentations of goal-setting procedures. Here are some of the groups of questions and topics which he thinks strategy makers should consider when defining a company's missions and long-range programs:

Charter
    Scope, purpose, and objectives
    Product-line concept, including unique values offered, directions
        of effort, and new aims
Position
    Industry structure and character
    Profit sources
    Life-cycle stages of products
    Market share and area
    Utilization of capacity
Attributes or Capabilities
    Strengths
    Weaknesses
Environment
    Outlook for market demand
    Competition and price
    Distribution channels
    Changing technology
    Trends in the economy
    Regulatory constraints
    Community constraints
Impact of Trends and Conditions on Company
    Problems and needs
    Threats
    Opportunities
Momentum of Present Operations
    Prospects and goals
    Premises
    Profit-and-loss summary
Programs of Action
    How should the company respond to challenges in the environ-
        ment?
    How should it respond to its present state of strengths and weak-
        nesses?
    What alternatives should be considered?
    How should resources be used for capital projects, geographical
        expansion, raw-material procurement, services, merchandis-

ing, acquisition of smaller companies, financial demands, and so on?

Technical Programs
  Support (cost reduction, product improvement, sales service, market development)
  Innovative projects
Organization
  What needs and plans should be considered?
Goals
  Sales
  Profits

Exhibit I reproduces a chart Smalter has used to show the interrelationships between different types of planning during the annual work cycle. (The lighter areas of the bars denote periods of secondary emphasis.)

Methods of Statement

How are goals stated? They may be stated in terms of activities, in financial terms, in terms of desired positions (like market share or quality leadership), or in combinations of such ways.

An illustration of the first method is a company which designed and made engine components for the military during World War II and the postwar period. When it ran into problems keeping this business profitable, its management began trying to formulate new goals for the company. It became especially interested in the prospect of developing original products in particular areas of advanced technology. To make this aim meaningful, a good deal of attention was paid to a combination of objectives: competence in certain design functions, for instance, plus development of sales forces in specified fields and proficiency in certain kinds of research. These latter might be called "subgoals" of the broad goals first decided on. (See discussion of the hierarchy of goals later in this chapter.)

In other companies, more attention is given to broad financial

Exhibit I. Annual Planning Calendar

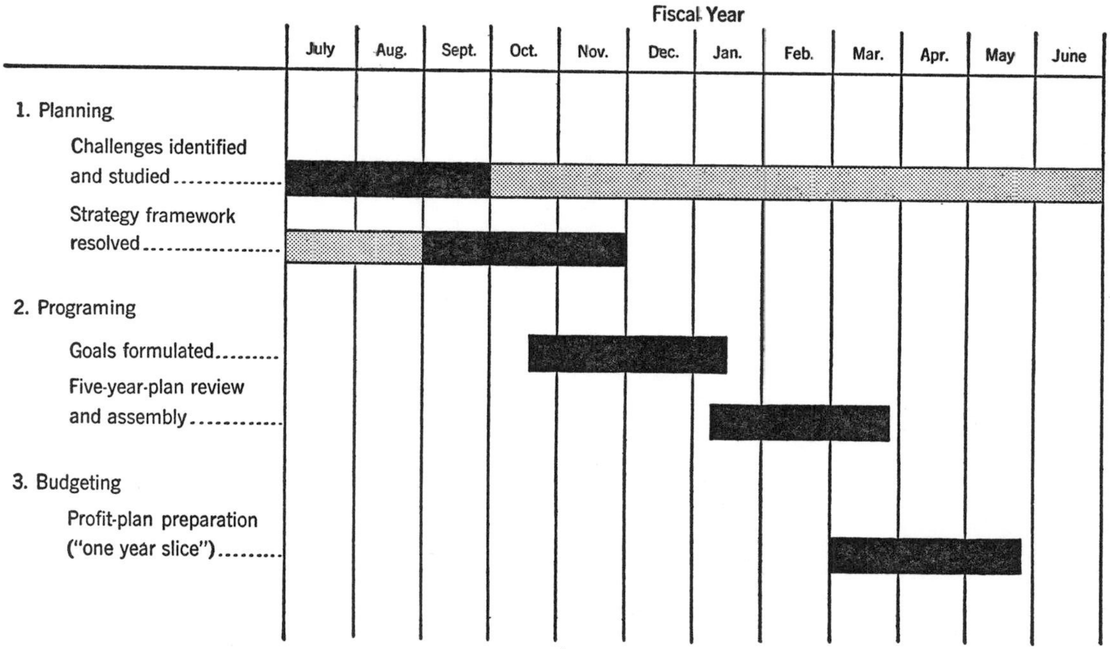

Fiscal Year

	July	Aug.	Sept.	Oct.	Nov.	Dec.	Jan.	Feb.	Mar.	Apr.	May	June

1. Planning

Challenges identified and studied ....

Strategy framework resolved ....

2. Programing

Goals formulated ....

Five-year-plan review and assembly ....

3. Budgeting

Profit-plan preparation ("one year slice") ....

corporate goals. For example, Ford Motor Company expresses over-all corporate goals in terms of expected increases in profits per share and specified rates of return on total assets. The first measure affords a kind of overview of corporate performance, while the second is useful for controlling revenues, costs, and the efficiency of operations. The second can also be broken down into individual return-on-assets figures for each division or subsidiary. The corporate finance staff discusses these targets with the division heads before recommending a final set of goals to the president and chairman for their approval.[1]

Main Characteristics

What are the characteristics of good strategic goals? First of all, as planning leaders have emphasized many times, they are *specific*. They are specific enough to help managers choose between different alternatives of action. An objective like "Increase sales 15 per cent" may be useful at times to the chairman of the board of directors, perhaps, but it does not provide guidance for the line executives who will be making decisions affecting sales. Increase sales in what fields or with what product lines? Increase sales at any cost—for example, lower profitability—or in conjunction with certain profit goals, too? Obviously, such matters must be taken up if any kind of coordinated management effort is to be achieved; there are as many ways to increase sales 15 per cent as there are to skin a cat, and different managers can be counted on to try them all.

Similarly, an objective like "Double the size of the organization" does not tell executives whether to expand sales and production in the current lines of business (and if so, in what order of priority), in new lines, or in some other way.

The only caveat here is that competent strategists do not make

---

[1] See *Corporate Planning Today*, A Business International Research Report (New York: Business International Corporation, July, 1964), pp. 57–58.

goals so specific that the broad "what to do" becomes "how to do it."

Second, good strategic goals have a *time dimension*. The significance of a goal like "Increase sales 15 per cent" varies considerably, depending on whether it is to be done by next year or within the next decade. This time dimension is not always precise, in cases where good planning is done, but it is definite enough in managers' minds so that it guides them in choosing courses of action.

How far ahead should planning, short-range and long-range, go? It is surprising that this question is raised as often as it is in discussions of planning, as if it had some significance of its own in decision making. I know of no case of good planning where management asked, "How far ahead shall we plan?" and answered that question before deciding on the content of the program. The question is useful sometimes in getting a good discussion started, because it leads to the more basic questions. But once those are settled, the question of time span can be answered routinely. Everything depends on how much of the future is affected by present decisions; that may be a long time (as in the steel industry) or a short time (as in fashion apparel). Within a large corporation, the time implications of present decisions may even vary greatly from department to department (for instance, 4–5 years for marketing and 10–15 years for finance).

Third, well-thought-out objectives are *consistent* with one another. If one objective is to increase sales volume by a certain amount and another is to increase profitability, they may well be in conflict. Are the opportunities to increase volume such that profitability can be increased, too? Or is it a case of having to elect one *or* the other, or both only so long as they can be kept in balance with each other? Some of the more subtle forms of conflict occur in product-line problems, where an expansion or contraction in one line will affect business in another. Indeed, if one subscribes to the role of a corporate image in determining consumer buying behavior, there is practically no act of price cutting, package changing, advertising revision, or quality manipulation in one product line that may not conceivably affect all others.

Fourth, objectives are based not just on facts but also on *values* and *feelings* about the facts. If a company is in what investors call the electronics industry, in which part of that industry should it be—industrial controls, consumer appliances, precision measurements, or what? Each part calls for different orders of risk taking as well as of know-how.

Several years ago Trans World Airlines was seeking (successfully, as it turned out) to reverse its sagging fortunes. "We had a decision to face early in the game," said the president, Charles C. Tillinghast, "as it became obvious that we were in a period of downswing. The question was: Should we cut costs and retrench first, or should we go all-out for fully competitive service? We concluded that a drastic retrenchment wasn't the way to win the battle in the long term."[2] A question like this does not get resolved by looking at the facts. Analyzing the facts will help, but the probe could go on forever without producing an answer. What facts do you look at? How do you weigh them? How do you relate them to one another? This is where value judgments come in, sometimes like a small nagging voice from the corner, at other times like a large and overbearing presence.

Fifth, there is a growing feeling in both the government and business communities that goals should be stated first in terms of *corporate-wide missions,* not of desired departmental or divisional programs independently formulated. The impetus for this trend came from the regime of Secretary Robert McNamara and his capable assistant Charles J. Hitch in the Department of Defense. Prior to their arrival in 1961, the Army, Navy, and Air Force made their programs and budgets with only minimal attention

2 *Forbes,* August 15, 1963, p. 13.

to each other's operations. Coordination was not ignored, but neither did it figure high in each department's strategic thinking. McNamara and Hitch set up a system of planning by missions which was done for DOD first as a whole unit and *then* translated into Army, Navy, and Air Force programs. For instance, "mission program packages" were established regarding nuclear retaliation capability, local crises where police forces were required, and so forth.

Sixth, goals are *hierarchical.* There are different levels of goals, proceeding from fairly broad and general aims to increasingly specific and departmentalized programs. A fine statement of this characteristic is made by Charles Granger. Under objectives of the "grand design" type (such as "We will build a telephone system so that anybody, anywhere, can talk with anyone else, anywhere in the world, quickly, cheaply, and satisfactorily") Granger puts in descending order:

- Missions in fulfillment of the grand design (e.g., strategic retaliation, for the Department of Defense)
- Charters or definitions of the business of operating units that support missions (e.g., manufacture and sale of small appliances, for a division in that industry)
- Policies or statements of common purpose (e.g., policies on management development)
- Desired results in key areas (e.g., a desired position in the market, or a desired rate of profitability)
- Long-range plans for given periods of time (e.g., a five-year plan for a staff unit)
- Strategic programs (e.g., a program for developing a mass market)
- Budgets (e.g., a budget for a particular operating unit)
- Short-term programs (e.g., a program for opening a new office).[3]

[3] "The Hierarchy of Objectives," *Harvard Business Review*, May–June, 1964, p. 66.

Steps for Implementation

A second major set of motions that organizations go through when they plan has to do with the steps, measures, and programs set up to achieve the broad goals. Authorities on planning have labeled this second set of motions in different ways. To contrast it with strategic planning (sometimes called comprehensive, over-all, or objectives planning), the second set is called variously tactical, derivative, functional, operational, or *implementational* planning. Almost all the experts agree that in a given organization there are more possibilities for delegating and spreading around decisions concerning implementational planning than strategic planning.

What general kinds of steps and procedures do managements direct when they go about implementing strategic plans? They must decide, of course, what the most essential tasks are and who should do them. They are likely to pay close attention to devices for coordinating these tasks, including information systems. Deadlines will probably be set for different jobs; and more and more, executives in progressive firms and agencies are talking about deciding in advance how to measure and evaluate performance. Incentives, rewards, penalties, and controls are also likely to get a fair share of attention.[4]

Among managers generally, there seems to be a distinct preference for implementational planning over strategic planning. In part this reflects the fact that strategic decisions are usually made by a relatively small group in a business or government organization, and in part the fact that a person normally has much more experience during his child and adult life with "how-to-do-it" decisions than with "goals" decisions. But there is another important reason that implementational planning is so often

---

[4] For an excellent discussion of these steps, see Edmund P. Learned, C. Roland Christensen, Kenneth R. Andrews, and William D. Guth, *Business Policy: Text and Cases* (Homewood, Ill.: Richard D. Irwin, 1965), pp. 619–631 and 684–704.

preferred. It is more specific, more concrete, more visible. When a manager works on the implementation of plans and programs, he thinks in terms of certain people, jobs, facilities—things that he knows and can see. Implementational planning is not so abstract as strategic planning. Its appeal to the manager is more visceral. And it satisfies the achievement motive more, for things happen in front of a manager's eyes when he works successfully on the execution of programs.

This is not to say that implementational planning comes easily. The point is simply that this type of planning in many organizations has a vitality and energy not so often seen with strategic planning. Of course, this only makes it all the more important to make strategic decisions well; otherwise, the organization may veer off course in a short time, like a bicycle zigzagging out of control. It also becomes more important to inquire into the possibility that there are ways of setting goals that will excite managers more and arouse a greater sense of commitment from them.

These observations lead us to the next chapters of this book—to some basic alternatives in setting goals, to the all-important question of relating future objectives to today's realities in an organization, and to the principal stages of strategy formulation.

The Outside-In Approach

4

The nature of strategic planning is more qualitative than quantitative. Statistics on market volume, profit opportunities, classes and numbers of people to be served, costs, and other matters are important, but the really decisive elements are the values, aspirations, and attitudes of managers and employees. Facing precisely the same situation, and basing their decisions on identical sets of figures, one college may decide to double its size in the long term while another decides not to increase its size at all; one health and welfare agency may elect to diversify its services while another plans no change whatever; one business may choose to revolutionize its product lines while another chooses to make only gradual adjustments. And the executives of each organization may be doing the right thing.

Strategic planning, therefore, concerns the way an organization elects to act in relation to needs and opportunities foreseen in its environment. It concerns the organization's efforts to collect information which will illuminate the best choice of action, to define problems and limitations in the way as well as opportunities and strengths, to define different basic approaches to a desired result and compare the merits of these approaches.

How does management go about doing these jobs? Not surprisingly, the best-known procedure emphasizes the continuous surveying, forecasting, and analyzing of the environment. Management begins by asking: What are the most significant market opportunities or public needs to be met? Second, management asks: In view of our organization's strengths and weaknesses, which of these opportunities or needs should we try to meet? Since the reasoning begins with external conditions and turns next to internal capacities and desires, I call this procedure the outside-in approach. It is a justly celebrated approach to goal setting. To convey the essence of it, let me offer a "pure" example, recognizing that in practice most applications of outside-in are not quite so extreme.

In the middle 1950's two bright young businessmen were looking for an opportunity to organize a new company. Although they were working at the time for different employers, they kept in touch with each other and had agreed on a general plan of action. They would wait until they found an opportunity to make a great deal of money and make it fast. To find such an opening, they would search first for a field of activity where a new venture was clearly needed—a field where there were plenty of prospective customers who were not already being served by existing organizations. Second, of course, the opportunity had to be one which was within their financial and personal abilities to exploit.

The two men considered a wide range of possibilities and finally settled on the shoe-repair business in Europe, South Africa, and Australia. By renting space in department stores and other areas where people were shopping, they would be able to bring their services right to the customer. They would give fast, fix-it-while-you-wait service (in contrast to the slow service in countries like Belgium, where it usually took three days to get a woman's shoe heel fixed). And they would apply modern work methods, accounting practices, and other business procedures.

Although one of the two men had worked in off hours on an improved shoe-repair machine, neither had any expertise in the shoe business or any aspect of it. One had been working for Kaiser Steel and U.S. Steel in the United States, the other for Procter & Gamble in Europe. But they did perceive accurately that there was a real need for the venture they were going to organize, and they saw no reason why they could not meet this need. In this sense, they were true followers of the marketing philosophy and in particular of the popular notion that the first principle of business strategy is to look to the market, to the customer, and see where the greatest needs for service lie.

This strategy paid off handsomely for D. Hillsdon Ryan and Donald W. Phillips. In 1957 they opened a "heel bar," as it was called, in the Brussels department store Au Bon Marché. It made money fast. By the end of 1958 their enterprise was operating six heel bars in Belgium and Switzerland; and early in 1966, *International Management* reported, they had five hundred quick-service stations going in Europe, Australia, and South Africa. Sales for 1966, the magazine added, were expected to reach $10 million.[1]

Rationale

When proponents explain why they favor the outside-in philosophy, they are likely to cite the dangers of *not* following it. They may point to the example of a company that got so enamored of a favorite product or service that it forgot what its main mission was—satisfying customers—or to the example of a firm that began with a good market but became inbred, bureaucratic, and incapable of adapting to customer desires as they changed in later years. As Theodore Levitt observes in a famous statement of marketing philosophy: "An industry begins with the customer and his needs, not with a patent, a raw material, or a selling skill. Given the customer's needs, the industry develops backwards, first concerning itself with the physical *delivery* of customer satisfactions. Then it moves back further to

[1] February, 1966, p. 69.

creating the things by which these satisfactions are in part achieved."[2]

In the case of an educational institution, outside-in would mean working back from the mission of teaching students to the arrangement of adequate facilities and the procurement of good teachers. In the case of a government agency—the Interstate Commerce Commission, let us say—outside-in would mean working back from the mission of assuring fast, safe, economical transportation for the public.

Outside-in supporters cite statements like the one attributed to Charles Kettering, the automobile industry leader. When asked in an interview whether he believed that "if a man made a better mousetrap, the world would make a beaten path to his door," he replied, "The people who have mice will!" The moral which seems unassailable is that any would-be seller of goods and services may waste his time completely if he does not check first to see if people want what he proposes to offer them; that any government seeking popular support had best examine the public need and desire for programs before undertaking them; that any educational organization should scrutinize trends and student requirements before planning courses and curricula.

The outside-in approach is also heralded as the antidote to the temptation to stay with a good thing too long. The fall of Underwood Corporation is perhaps the classic illustration of this danger. In 1937, Underwood had almost exactly the same sales volume that International Business Machines did: $30 million. But while IBM and other office machine companies kept plowing their earnings back into their businesses, Underwood maintained one of the highest pay-out rates in the industry; over 85 per cent of its net income went out in cash dividends year after year. And while IBM and other competitors took advantage of World War II defense contracts to learn new technologies that were developing (for instance, electronics), Underwood produced rifles. Then it turned down a chance to pioneer the electric typewriter.

2 "Marketing Myopia," *Harvard Business Review,* July–August, 1960, p. 55.

When, in the 1950's, it belatedly tried to get into the computer business in order to stay competitive, it was too late. In 1959, once-great Underwood had to sell control to Olivetti.[3]

One of many strong arguments for outside-in thinking is that in our technologically oriented economy, the researcher, the engineer, and the production man, who naturally have a strong voice in business policy, tend to be product- and process-oriented rather than customer-oriented. They become engrossed in technical perfection, forgetting that the customer often does not care about that at all, especially if a different way of meeting his wants is offered from another source. In "Marketing Myopia," therefore, Levitt cautions leaders in electronics and chemicals not to take the seeming invulnerability of their industries for granted. He urges them not to forget that their customers, too, can go the way of so many other markets in the past. It may be hard for them right now to see how things can ever go wrong in their galloping industries, he notes, but "They probably also cannot see how a reasonably sensible businessman could have been as myopic as the famous Boston millionaire who 50 years ago unintentionally sentenced his heirs to poverty by stipulating that his entire estate be forever invested exclusively in electric streetcar securities. His posthumous declaration, 'There will always be a big demand for efficient urban transportation,' is no consolation to his heirs who sustain life by pumping gasoline at automobile filling stations."[4]

Leading Varieties

Like any influential concept, the outside-in philosophy has come to mean somewhat different things to different management groups over the years. This indeed is one of the philosophy's strengths. What are the most important varieties and forms that are practiced?

[3] *Forbes*, July 1, 1963, p. 15.
[4] Theodore Levitt, "Marketing Myopia," *op. cit.*, p. 47.

First and most obvious, outside-in describes the all-out efforts many companies make to capitalize on market forecasts (and the efforts many noncommercial organizations make to capitalize on public opinion or needs forecasts). A case in point is Mobile Home Manufacturers Association, a Chicago-based company which has been strikingly successful in producing and selling trailers. According to managing director Edward L. Wilson, "We have grown by filling a vacuum, time after time." In World War II the vacuum was military housing; the postwar vacuum was family housing and college dormitories; more recent vacuums have been housing for retired people who do not like to live in apartments and young married couples who want to acquire their own homes and furniture cheaply in one main purchase.[5] Management has been making a special effort to size up these vacuums before they become obvious and move in to fill them efficiently before competitors can.

Continental Casualty Company is applying much the same approach in insurance. This company, known as "Lloyd's of Chicago," boasts a number of "firsts" in its industry; for instance, it was the first insurance company to sell policies against polio on a national scale and the first to sell group dental insurance. Today, one of its reported long-term goals is package insurance —a policy that will cover everything that could possibly happen to a man, his family, and his possessions. "It still is a long way off," stated Chairman Howard C. Reeder, "but the day is coming when an insurance company will be able to say to a customer: 'For X dollars, we'll insure you, period.' "[6] Here again, a management is building its strategy on the basis of unfilled needs that it sees developing.

Still another example of the same general approach is American Metal Climax, Inc., called in early 1965 the United States' most profitable major metals company. Amax executives, it was reported at that time, analyzed the prospects of the metals in-

[5] *Forbes*, March 15, 1965, p. 35.
[6] *Forbes*, February 1, 1965, p. 36.

dustry and concluded that, competition notwithstanding, aluminum would continue to be the fastest-growing major metal. They predicted, too, that there would be room for new competitors. On this basis, they were committing the company to a very substantial investment in aluminum production (previously the company had held merely a fringe position in this field). If their predictions were wrong, Chairman Walter Hochschild stated, "we'll have made a big mistake." Thus, although another feature of the company's strategy was to stick to areas compatible with its skills and experience, the really dynamic factor in its decision making was market forecasting.

A *second* variety of the outside-in approach, closely related to the foregoing, is practiced by managements emphasizing the benefits of riding on growth-industry waves. In the mid-sixties a leading management magazine published an article called "What Makes a Growth Company?"[7] Eight criteria of such a company were listed. One was: "Operate in high growth segment(s) of economy." Another was: "A corporate structure organized for responsiveness to opportunities." The thinking seems to be that if management can keep the organization moving into those markets which are expanding and deepening, it will give the company the best chance to grow and expand.

Third, the outside-in concept has been used by shrewd executives to direct efforts to supplement and balance the kinds of business a company is in. For instance, Emerson Electric Company has been primarily a manufacturer of electric motors, drives, controls, light fixtures, heating apparatus, and so forth. Its major diversification effort has been in the defense industry. To raise its level of sales from defense contracts and gain corporate balance (even though defense contracts were not as profitable as electric apparatus), Chairman Wallace R. Persons in 1964 asked Arthur D. Little, Inc., to help him select six promising areas of defense work into which to try to expand.[8] The

[7] *Dun's Review and Modern Industry*, October, 1964.
[8] *Forbes*, March 1, 1965, p. 18.

decision to expand into these areas (including antisubmarine electronics and heat shields for space craft) was based largely on technological forecasts.

Fourth, outside-in characterizes some managements' philosophy of diversification by acquisition. These are the management groups that use reported profits as the first criterion of desirability, ahead of (although not excluding) such other criteria as complementariness of product line or research potential. An illustration is the strategy of International Silver Company, a century-old firm which is the world's largest silversmith. It became convinced, in the 1950's, that if it were to grow, it would have to go into fields outside the silverware business. It set out on a program of corporate buying, picking up controlling interests in such firms as Times Wire and Cable, Eyelet Specialties (cosmetic containers), Eastwood-Neally (wire screen), and W. H. Hutchinson (bottle caps). The firms acquired had little in common with one another except that their return on sales or investment was better than what International Silver was getting. In effect, therefore, management was basing its purchases on what the market was already telling it about the profitability and profit potential of various companies.

Fifth, outside-in thinking in some companies means placing special emphasis on industry economic trends in strategic decision making. For instance, National Can Corporation, of Chicago, came to the conclusion, in the mid-1950's, that there was no place in the United States economy for a small can maker. Although National Can was the third largest manufacturer of metal containers, it had less than 4 per cent of the market. Its six plants could supply only packers who were located in the plant areas; hence the company could not really be called a "national" can company. Also, circumstances in the industry were such that a small can company had especially tough seasonal sales problems to solve. For these reasons, President Robert S. Solinsky and his management team undertook an ambitious, aggressive expansion program. Can companies in different areas were purchased; although profitability declined, sales volume rose from $41 million in 1954 to $147 million in 1964.[9] Here again, the character of the motive was basically outside-in: the crucial factor, as management saw it, was what the industry environment required the company to do in order to survive.

Sixth, the outside-in approach characterizes much government planning. As one example, in the 1950's Washington authorized a highway program carrying commitments that extended into 1972. The program was laid out and sold to Congress on the basis of studies of highway needs in the years ahead; relatively little attention was given to the total needs or resources of government. Again, the "missions" which the Department of Defense decided on a few years ago—nuclear retaliation ability, for instance, and capacity to fight local wars—were formulated completely on the basis of what capabilities Pentagon experts thought would be necessary if the United States was going to maintain its position as a world power second to none. Smaller countries would not have been able to proceed in this way. They would have had to weigh their aspirations against their strengths and resources, eliminating some desirable "missions" from the picture.

To cite another example, in England architects and town planners are working out goals for building design and regional transportation on the basis of predictions of what conditions will be like in the year 2000 A.D. They see 18 million more people in Britain; they foresee more leisure; they expect certain advances in transportation and communication. On the basis of this picture of their world thirty-five years hence, they are trying to decide today what Britain should look like tomorrow. Note, once more, acceptance of the forecast environment as a "given" and emphasis on working back from the expected future to the present rather than vice versa.

Seventh, outside-in often characterizes strategies where government-business relationships are paramount. If, for example, a

[9] *Forbes*, March 15, 1965, p. 42.

corporation feels that it is vulnerable to antitrust action, it may rule out expansion by acquiring other companies, or it may avoid entering into joint ventures with other companies, even if the opportunities therefrom would be great. Again, there are some people in the pharmaceutical industry who believe that much could be gained by larger investments in fundamental research, not so much because of the practical value of the knowledge to be gained (although that might be considerable) as because of its public relations value. Such research could be used to justify the high margins and returns the industry receives. These returns have been called unconscionably high in Congressional hearings. In both cases, strategy is dictated first and most influentially by judgments about outside trends and conditions.

An *eighth* variety of the outside-in approach is patterning an organization's structure, operations, or management style after those found elsewhere in industry. Not long ago White Motor Company attempted to merge with Cummins Engine, but the Justice Department refused to allow the deal to go through. The top management of White Motor was left with a strategic problem to solve: it had to grow from within, if it were to grow (which seemed economically necessary), but growing from within meant competing with such industrial giants as General Motors and International Harvester. How could a small company compete effectively with organizations having such vast resources? Management's answer was that it would have to begin operating the way some well-known large companies operated. It set up a research group on the West Coast, well separated from the operating pressures of headquarters. It organized an international division. And it brought in about fifteen outside staff experts to study and advise operating executives on personnel, marketing, manufacturing, and engineering. "When we were a small company," the president said, "I used to get most of the studies together myself."[10]

10 *Forbes*, February 15, 1965, p. 29.

Identifying Characteristic

These eight varieties of the outside-in approach will strike most observers as reflecting differences of degree rather than of substance. The differences may be quite important to the various companies practicing them, but they are not significant from a conceptual point of view. Outside-in thinking always emphasizes fitting the organization to the market or public need, adapting to anticipated opportunity, responding to external change. Its trade-mark is the primacy of the forecast. It centers the attention of management on opportunities that events are creating—events in the market place, in economic development, or in national and international affairs.

An outside-in strategy is not, of course, molded *solely* by forecasts (except in the case of Department of Defense "missions"). As authorities have repeatedly stated, the strengths, weaknesses, and desires of the organization are taken into account, too. But the forecast is the cornerstone, the beginning point. And it is the most dynamic element in the mix of factors.

Potentials—and Potholes

The outside-in approach to strategic goal setting has some stunning advantages. For one thing, it engenders alertness, aggressiveness, foresightedness. When Joseph C. Wilson, president of Xerox, refused to be complacent with that company's enormous success in the mid-1960's and insisted on programs for branching out into new areas—"If you don't diversify, you can disappear," he said—he was reflecting a kind of restless discontent which is often associated with outside-in thinking. When some shrewd entrepreneurs in Japan started up coffeehouses in that country in 1965, despite the protests of less imaginative people that "you can't sell coffee to the Japanese; they want tea," they demonstrated a kind of imagination often associated with outside-in. They were amply rewarded for deciding that it was about time the Japanese were exposed to coffee, for by early 1966 coffee was the "in" drink in Japan and coffeehouses were hot properties there.

Outside-in also encourages managers to take a broad view of the role of their organizations. Late in 1965 Leonard F. Mc-Collum, chairman of Houston's Continental Oil Company, made a deal with Chairman George Love of Consolidation Coal Company to buy "Consol." The purchase made the United States' ninth biggest oil company the biggest coal company as well. But size and power were not the main rationale of the deal. For McCollum was thinking in energy terms, as opposed to petroleum terms. With this broader, more visionary sense of mission, he saw the advantages of vastly expanding Continental's energy base. This, too, is a way of thinking quite characteristic of the outside-in philosophy.

Of course, there are various other advantages. Outside-in tends to bring out latent strengths in an organization—to challenge management to exploit capacities that it might not have appreciated otherwise. A classic example of this is one of George Borg's early achievements with the clutch.[11] In the 1920's his plant (later to become part of Borg-Warner Corporation) made clutches for midwestern automobile manufacturers. Studying industry trends, Borg became convinced that it would be imperative, if his plant were to survive, to produce a clutch that would do the job at half the present price. When he told his engineers this, they were aghast; it was out of the question. His father, part owner of the company, scoffed at the idea, too. Cut clutches out like cookies on a punch press? Nonsense! But Borg persisted, driven by his conviction that the market demanded the change. He called a conference of his engineers, after some time had elapsed, to see what progress they had made on his idea. They

---

[11] This story, taken from Robert J. Casey's biography, *Mr. Clutch*, is recounted in more detail in David W. Ewing, *The Managerial Mind* (New York: The Free Press, 1964), pp. 116–117.

said they had gone into it thoroughly and concluded that it could not be done. Borg said, "Then I'll have to get some fellows in here who can." The engineers agreed to try again. Borg told them on the way out, "And try harder." They did. And they found they *could* make a good clutch at half the price. This story typifies what has happened a great many times in organizational history as a result of outside-in decisions concerning what *needs* to be done regardless of whether, at the moment, it seems practical and possible to do.

Despite its merits, outside-in has disadvantages. They by no means discredit the approach. But they suggest that outside-in, like any other system of strategic planning, is not so glamorous in practice as in theory and that for a good many companies its impressive potentials are partly surrounded by pitfalls and potholes.

The first pothole is a subjective one. It concerns planning attitudes, managerial psychology, habits of mind. The danger, in a word, is "other-directedness." This term comes, of course, from the behaviorists, who use it to describe the individual who does what he does because he thinks it is expected of him by others. In organizational life, other-directedness means "following the leader." It means that an executive team seeks change in this way or that because (or partly because) other management groups are changing that way. It means that a college establishes such-and-such a curriculum because other respected colleges have established it. It means that governments set up procedures or missions of a certain kind because governments in other admired countries have set them up. Outside-in encourages other-directedness because it tempts managements to think of opportunities and needs as independent quantities, as having a separate existence of their own, and hence as being equally attractive to all.

For the organization, as for the individual, other-directedness may lead to that safety and acceptance which management wants. But sometimes—and especially in a competitive business system— it produces a contrary result. For instance, if one company diversifies into a certain field because its competitors are going there, or for the same reasons its competitors have so diversified, there is an excellent chance that the very popularity of the move will ruin its attractiveness. What may once have been virgin territory is quickly defoliated.

An interesting case in point is reported by *Printer's Ink*.[12] Not long ago, a number of distillers reached similar conclusions about the American liquor market. They saw the public reaching for more expensive products and desiring to experiment with different types of drinks. Seagram Distillers Company, which had once boasted only three brands in its line, saw Scotch becoming very popular, and the demand for bourbon, vodka, rums, and liqueurs increasing, too. "We've got to participate in this change," Seagram said. And it did, with some fine new brands. But its competitors were doing the same thing. When they all had made their moves, one top executive moaned, "Competition is fantastic now. It's just plain murder." It appeared that the new marketing strategy would pay off only for the few. The combination of opportunity plus *average* capability would not be enough to assure success.

The petrochemicals field, once highly touted as an unusual growth industry, was entered by so many major oil companies, and made the object of expansion by so many chemical companies, that declining prices and overcapacity disappointed many of the producers. The plastics industry was also seen once as a lucrative growth field. And for many firms it was, for a short time. But too many chemical, oil, automobile, appliance, metal, and other producers had the same idea. The high-profit stratum of the industry was quickly mined out, and only the fittest companies continued to find promising opportunities.

Another pothole in the outside-in approach concerns forecasting. Almost every organization in a changing world must make forecasts and use them in its planning. The trouble is that outside-in calls for uncommon finesse (or uncommon luck) in forecasting. It demands unusual sophistication and precision in

[12] "Shake-up in Liquor Market," January 28, 1966.

predicting markets and needs, in the timing of them as well as in judging their breadth and depth. Is it realistic to expect the majority of organizations to possess this skill? Judging from a wide range and growing proliferation of examples, the answer is no.

A case that has been talked about frequently is shipbuilding. In the old days, a shipbuilder's competition came from other shipbuilders. He could afford the attitude attributed to one leader in the industry: "Shipbuilding is such an old art that most of its development has been wrung out of it."[13] But by 1966 the creative thrust in shipbuilding was coming not from established builders like Newport News, Bath Iron Works, and American Shipbuilding, but from a wholly unanticipated source: aerospace companies like Aerojet-General, Lockheed, Grumman, Litton Industries, Bell Aerosystems, Boeing, and General Dynamics. These were the organizations that were coming forth with the hovercraft, the hydrofoil, and other variations that portended a transformation in the industry.

In retrospect, one may argue that the old-line shipbuilders should have anticipated this development. Perhaps they might have—with extraordinary forecasters and marketers. But is it *reasonable* to expect that men in these organizations could have got such good evidence of likely future developments, and presented it so persuasively to managers up and down the line, that they could have initiated changes in strategy on this basis?

Shipbuilding is not the only example, and perhaps not the best one. Take the cement industry. The competition that cement manufacturers are getting from producers of asphalt road-building materials is considered as important as that from other cement producers.[14] Forecasters say it is difficult enough to predict innovations that are forthcoming from one's immediate competi-

---

[13] *Forbes*, April 15, 1965.

[14] Edmund P. Learned, C. Roland Christensen, Kenneth R. Andrews, and William D. Guth, *Business Policy: Text and Cases* (Homewood, Ill.: Richard D. Irwin, 1965), p. 173.

tors; but what happens when firms in other industries must be kept on the radarscope, too?

There is nothing new about interindustry competition; it has been going on for some years. As Jay W. Forrester has pointed out, the electric razor did not come from the safety razor companies; the airplane was not designed by automobile companies; electronic computers did not get launched by the calculating machine or punched-card machine companies; atomic bombs and proximity fuses did not come from military research laboratories; and to a considerable extent, rockets and ballistic missiles did not come from organizations in the aircraft industry. The point is: competition from unexpected sources (or, at least, unexpected at the time they happen; in retrospect, they always seem to have been predictable!) seems to be accelerating. Of all people, strategy makers should be the last to overlook this. It reduces their ability to forecast accurately.

In the leather business, after the Great Depression, firms might well have expected the biggest innovation to be due in tanning methods. Some hard and intelligent work was going into that investigation; it must have seemed the most likely possibility for change. But the really striking new development came from outside the industry in the form of vinyls, synthetic rubber, new synthetics, Corfam. In the graphic arts, who has come forth with the most important innovations? Not leaders in that field, but firms working on electronic methods and applications of plastics. Or take the paper industry. Donald Schon tells that when he was with the Bureau of Standards he once discussed with members of a large paper company what the major innovation in paper had been in the past twenty to thirty years. Did they tell him it was faster Fourdrinier machines, new coating methods, better ways of handling the "white water" problem? No. The most important innovation they reported was polyethylene; for instance, waterproof polyethylene bags.

Was it feasible for a company in the textile industry, years ago, to foresee the development of nylon? It would have required forecasting gifts that few companies seem to have. Was it feasible for a firm in the machine-tool business in, say, 1914 to foresee that research on an antitank weapon in World War I would lead to the development of carbide tools, and in the 1930's, that World War II would create a demand for such machines that would greatly alter the state of the art of machine-tool building? Could firms in the industry reasonably have been expected, in the late 1940's and 1950's, to conceive that the next major innovation would be numerical controls, originally conceived by a midwesterner making helicopter rotor blades, developed by the Instrumentation Laboratory at MIT, and brought into production by Boeing?[15]

In the electronics industry, solid-state physics seems to be the major revolutionary force. In the housing industry, as well as in metals and packaging, plastics seems to be the most dynamic new influence. Again, to foresee the competitive thrust would have required looking in unlikely directions—or, at least, in what most reasonable men at the time would have considered to be unlikely and implausible directions.

Of course, what is true in industry is true in many fields outside of industry as well. Take psychology. Some dramatic advances seem to be in the offing today. Are they coming from researchers in psychoanalytic theory, as one might reasonably expect? No; they are coming from research in chemistry.

These difficulties of predicting technological change do not argue against forecasting. Far from it. Technological forecasting is assuming unprecedented importance. What they do argue for is the impracticality, for most companies, of using a forecast as the *starting place* in strategy. They argue for great humility on the part of decision makers who would try to outline the shape of things to come so clearly and accurately that they can justify choosing a precise strategy for the organization on the basis of this information.

15 Donald A. Schon, address to the Third Annual Michigan Industry–University Research Conference, October 21, 1964.

Market prediction is complicated further in today's advanced economy by the *transiency* of market conditions. Even if a company succeeds in predicting with accuracy the nature of an opportunity in the market place, it has not got over the hurdle. It must still possess the insight or marvelous good luck to see that that opportunity will not come and go in the twinkling of an annual profit-and-loss statement, as so many others have done before it.

For example, after World War II a candy manufacturer established some retail stores and profited handsomely from them. But these fat earnings were to be short-lived. When sugar rationing ended and a buyers' market returned, he went bankrupt because of these stores.[16] He saw an opportunity clearly and exploited it efficiently, but he did not foresee that conditions would change so fast.

The organization considering use of the outside-in approach should ask itself this question, too: How precisely can we tell in advance what our immediate competitors are capable of doing? Consider the case of Aluminium Limited. Prior to the 1950's, the top management of this great corporation worked out an imaginative and ambitious grand design: Aluminium would devote itself to becoming the lowest-cost aluminum producer in the world. During World War II it financed an enormous expansion in the Quebec wilderness, where hydroelectric power was abundant. Its cheaper power and closeness to low-cost water transportation seemed destined to give it an unbeatable chance to become mass ingot producer to the world. But management had underestimated its competitors. Reynolds managed to buy relatively low-cost power under long-term contracts; Kaiser built a new smelter in the Appalachian coal fields to get power at low cost. Both successes were unexpected. Then the United States firms moved into Aluminium's big overseas markets; Reynolds even succeeded in teaming up with a British firm to win control of British

16 Edmund P. Learned *et al.*, *op. cit.*, p. 28.

Aluminium, the largest fabricator of aluminum in that country. As overproduction grew and Aluminium lost customers to rival companies, it was forced to change the grand design that once seemed infallible.

To widen the forecasting pothole even more, there is the simple workaday difficulty of quantifying forecasts accurately. Everything may run in the company's favor except the practicality of hanging accurate profit-potential tags on a proposed project. Is there a $1 million market there or a $10 million one? Will it mature in two years or five years? In his study of planning in large companies, Norman Berg quotes one thoughtful vice-president as follows:

> I'm afraid that future profitability is simply too difficult to evaluate when dealing with decisions of this type. The most we can do is to list a number of factors which we think are indications of future profitability, and perhaps gather some information on some of them. We don't have any analytical way of taking all of these factors into account or combining them with each other—it will simply have to be a matter of discussion and judgment. We have a lot of abstract and unquantifiable factors to deal with, and someone will just have to decide. I do think that opportunities for profits in various fields are likely to depend heavily on growing markets and on high and rapidly changing technologies, but I don't think we have a good enough way of quantifying and working with these factors yet.[17]

An Evaluation

The outside-in approach seems to have proved itself best in these cases:

1. Companies with unusual marketing strengths. Because of their superior attunement to the market, they are able to move faster and more surely than competitors. They may not always have the best production and distribution systems, but they go in the right directions, and they get there first. The rich and volumi-

---

[17] "Strategic Planning in Conglomerate Companies," *Harvard Business Review*, May–June, 1965, p. 90.

nous literature on efficient marketing can be viewed as an effort to get more executives to think in these terms. This is fine. The rub is that, no matter how well the writers and teachers succeed, only the minority of companies can be above average and hence enjoy the extra margin.

2. Situations where a market is disappearing so surely and irretrievably that there is no point in listening to any voice except the marketing voice. The sooner one sees the handwriting on the market wall, in this case, and the more quickly he turns a deaf ear to production, research, accounting, and other pleas to stay put, the better off he will be.

3. Certain situations where the economics of the industry or the realities of government-business relationships are such that they override all other considerations. The situation in which National Can found itself (see pages 39–40) is an example of this; another example is the company with unusually severe antitrust problems on its hands if it pursues certain otherwise desirable growth strategies.

4. Various organizations in government, such as the Department of Defense and the Department of the Interior. When there is a clear, indisputable mission to perform (such as provision for national security or adequate forest land), and management has the resources at hand to perform it, then the best procedure is to look outward, identify the need clearly, and work back from that point to decide how best to meet it with various possible programs.

The Inside-Out Approach

5

By its actions an organization can often create a market, need, or opportunity which would not otherwise exist and which market analysts may not be able to foresee. This is the principle behind a second major method of choosing strategic goals.

How is such a market or opportunity created? Management looks first at the most important abilities, talents, and aptitudes of the organization—the abilities that give it some measure of advantage or superiority over other organizations in the field of attention. Next management considers the possibilities of strengthening these abilities: what might be done to build them up and improve the margin of superiority. Finally management looks outside the organization at the market or field of need, and it asks where the best opportunities lie for utilizing the organization's special strengths. Not until this relatively late stage does forecasting or economic analysis come in (although the reasoning process tends to be more circular than linear, with strategists repeating the cycle in their thinking and discussions). Instead of deferring the appraisal of strengths and weaknesses until after markets and missions are evaluated, as described in Chapter 4, management begins with that analysis.

To contrast the new procedure with the outside-in method, I call it the inside-out approach. It leads to different results from outside-in because of the different role assigned to forecasting. It also leads managers to place different priorities on the information-gathering process so important in strategic planning; information about organizational strengths and weaknesses, instead of being a kind of check or limiting factor, as in outside-in, becomes a crucial starting point which sets the whole tenor and scope of strategic analysis. The process of finding alternatives, also a common denominator of all varieties of strategic planning, becomes different, too, for inside-out will lead management to search more intensively in certain areas for alternative goals and programs.

Leading from Strength

Although the inside-out approach has received little formal attention in the literature and in discussion, and although it seems to contradict some sacred tenets of the marketing philosophy (the inconsistencies are likely to be exaggerated, as we shall see later), it has led a number of companies to remarkable successes. Let us look briefly at two examples, chosen deliberately from widely contrasting industries and situations, which show why inside-out is at the opposite end of the spectrum from the outside-in method.

An Insurance Company

The postwar success of Franklin Life Insurance Company, stated *Forbes*, "has become something of an industry legend."[1] Franklin Life's strategy was to deliberately emphasize only ordinary life policies; it decided to steer clear of group, industrial, and accident and health insurance. Moreover, it decided to offer only a limited number of package policies. It put tremendous

[1] April 15, 1964, p. 24.

stress on the salesman. As George E. Hatmaker, the president, explained: "There are no patents in this business. Any company can issue the same kinds of policies as another. The difference is in the people who are selling them."

When these goals were set, early in the postwar period, management was acting contrary to "the book." What would have been called for by most outside-inners, at least, was diversification into the new growth areas of the insurance business. This was what many leading firms were already doing, seeking in this manner to hedge their bets and also avoid the danger of getting stampeded in the most conventional, most competitive battleground of the industry. They also sought, as the marketing man would have pointed out, to buy shares in the new, more imaginative parts of the industry where growth prospects seemed most attractive.

The heads of Franklin Life did not see it this way. They believed they knew how to hire and supervise salesmen who could excel at selling straight life policies with no frills or alternatives. They believed they could do this better than most or all other competitors. And when, with this conviction in mind, they looked at trends in the industry, they decided that *for them* it made sense to concentrate in this narrow line—that if they did so with the skills they thought they could bring to bear, great opportunities would open up for them. Their strategy proved to be sound. During the 1950's many life insurance companies found the going rough, approached the break-even point, and decided to take a capital gain; by the early 1960's, the number merging or selling out was almost as great as the number of new firms being established. But Franklin Life's sales, during this period, climbed steadily and rapidly. Insurance in force rose over 1,300 per cent in 20 years—from $447 million in 1946 to $6.5 billion in 1966.

An Electronics Company

In Harrisburg, Pennsylvania, the policy makers of an electronics company, though faced with a radically different product problem, were thinking in similar terms. AMP Incorporated (formerly Aircraft-Marine Products) was charting its course in an industry which was becoming one of the most competitive ones in the United States; by the early 1960's some four thousand companies of all shapes and sizes were struggling against one another for customers. AMP was a supplier of terminals and connectors to the electrical and electronics industries. Its sales in 1952 were around $15 million, decidedly less than the sales of many competitors. What should its strategy be?

Outside-in strategists almost surely would have urged diversification. They would have warned against concentration. If the company happened to succeed in its narrow area, they would have argued, it would then attract larger, more powerful competitors and be crowded out. Besides, electronics was a fast-growing industry, and the place for a smart company to be was in the forefront of the new technologies. It was therefore necessary to pick out the most promising growth areas, decide which ones were best matched to the company's abilities, and expand into them. This was surely the sound course according to "the book."

If such advice was given AMP, it was rejected. Management believed that if it could mass its technical, financial, and marketing strength in a very narrow field, it could offer a line of highly engineered, custom-tailored products that few competitors could match. "We engineer the hell out of our products," chairman and founder Uncas A. Whitaker remarked. "In my book, one top engineer is worth 100 average engineers."[2] The research, development, and engineering budget was pegged at an average 12 to 13 per cent of sales. The philosophy followed was Bernard Baruch's one of "Put all your eggs in one basket and watch the basket carefully." Some new products were added, but they fell into the same area of specialized electromechanical know-how as terminals and conductors.

Although such a strategy would have struck outside-inners as

[2] *Forbes*, August 15, 1963.

suicide, it paid off handsomely. Sales rose to more than $140 million in 1966, and net income per share rose steadily from 27 cents in 1955 to $2.05 in 1965. If a company must have extraordinary skill in engineering and managing a narrow product line in order to avoid the usual dangers of specialization, AMP had that skill. Turning from this strength to the market, management could see that there was more potential there than many a market analyst might have thought.

The inside-out approach does not necessarily lead a company to stay in the same industry (though that happened in the foregoing illustrations). It may well point the way into very different industries and areas of effort. This happens when the organization has talents and abilities that would serve it usefully in new fields even though it has no operating experience in them.

Inside-out has its shortcomings and limitations, as we shall see, but it has one overriding advantage to compensate for these: it leads an organization to work on the kinds of project and program which employees have demonstrated real capacity to handle —programs where they can feel confident they will excel, programs they can have real enthusiasm for. It is partly because of this morale factor that the approach may produce results that exceed the predictions of market researchers and industry analysts.

Formulating an Inside-Out Strategy

Having taken this bird's-eye look at inside-out, let us make a closer examination of its practical operation. The example I shall use comes from actual corporate experience, although certain facts are disguised to protect the company's identity.

The company produced communications equipment of advanced types. Its top executives had backgrounds in science or engineering, although they no longer considered themselves "experts" in these areas after having devoted most of their time for some years to administration. Almost from its inception, the company had operated successfully. Sales volume rose steadily from a few hundred thousand dollars to quite a few million; net earnings had almost always been satisfactory; and debt obligations had always been easily met. Over half of the stock was publicly owned.

During the first few years of planning, the work was done on an informal basis, with few written documents, but even during that period the chief executive and others were "planning minded." These managers felt uneasy about the organization's dependence on a few large industrial customers, especially when technology was changing as fast as it was in the late 1950's and early 1960's, and they considered planning a necessity in view of the uncertainties. Not surprisingly, planning became more formal as time went on, and one of the vice-presidents was assigned almost 100 per cent to planning responsibilities. In general, the steps he followed for working out formal programs, especially long-range programs, were about the same as those described in many articles and books: establishment of broad goals first, then more specific objectives, and then the development of sales forecasts, financial forecasts, and programs for specific functions as needed (manufacturing, personnel, purchasing, and so on).

Several years ago the company undertook certain strategic moves. At the time these moves were first considered there was, thanks to earlier thinking ahead, a general consensus among top executives that the company should continue to develop and expand its technical output, that some kind of diversification was needed for the sake of stability, and that every effort should be made to stay in the forefront of communications technology in whatever areas were served. There was general agreement that the organization had advanced abilities at problem solving and had the financial ability to expand and diversify, but that it was "thin" in middle management and staff services, short on plant space, and not particularly adept in many marketing functions.

As management appreciated, these general notions about goals, strengths, and weaknesses fell far short of providing answers for strategic planning. The chief executive and the planning vice-president agreed to hold a series of management meetings on these questions. To get executives' thinking started well in advance, they worked out an agenda for the meetings. One of the most important parts of this agenda was a series of questions concerning the present status of the organization. For instance, managers were asked to ponder the organization's technical capabilities in all fields in which it was engaged: where specifically it seemed to excel, where performance was average, where the record showed weaknesses. Again, managers were asked to size up the company's manufacturing abilities: its know-how in quality control, reliability methods, value analysis, and the like. They also were asked to analyze managerial strengths and weaknesses in various departments, single out the most important positive factors in bringing the company to its present position, identify the salient retarding factors, and examine other topics.

In addition, managers were asked to consider what projects and programs they thought the company should undertake during the next four years. It was specified they should select projects which would take full advantage of the organization's talents and resources and would exercise these talents further. Also, the projects proposed should be consistent with the general corporate goals of expansion, stability through diversification, and technological leadership.

As might be expected, there were marked differences in various men's views of corporate strengths and weaknesses and of desirable program areas. But consensus was reached on a number of important points, and much useful information was presented. On the basis of all this, the chief executive and the planning vice-president began shaping a preliminary list of projects, ventures, and programs.

Management then turned to a new phase: forecasting, marketing, and economics. The president himself participated in some of the market studies undertaken. The purpose of this phase, he made clear, was to assess market trends, technological trends, and opportunities for profits in the areas of the various project proposals. The object was to find which projects promised the greatest return on investment. When the projects were thus characterized, further discussions were held and a final program was agreed on. The company would move as soon as it could into a completely new area of communications technology, one which had just opened up as a result of scientific discovery and would require a pioneering research and development program. Second, the company would go into production of a specialized type of materials-handling equipment. This was an industry where the company had no prior experience, but the niche selected seemed well suited to its technical and service capabilities.

What about the project proposals which were ruled out? Some of them were cut because they appeared likely to impose excessive financial burdens on the corporation; they would call for so much investment and working capital that the organization might find itself "over its head" in financial obligations. Other proposals were rejected because the marketing opportunities did not seem great enough or appeared too uncertain. Interestingly enough, however, the market for the materials-handling venture was uncertain in many ways, too. The difference was that in this case there was a strong feeling that demand *could be created* once the new product line was offered. Still other proposals were eliminated from the plan because of the conviction they would overload functions where the organization was weak or had only average ability.

In sum, this company took an inside-out approach to strategic planning. It should be noted that marketing analysis was by no means eliminated, but only postponed in the sequence of activities. When management did turn its attention to forecasts and industry trends, it invested much time and effort in making them, with the president personally participating. While the focus of attention was on positive talents and resources, organizational weaknesses also were brought into the picture and played a part in finalizing the plan.

The strategy turned out to be successful; the company fared well in both of the new ventures. To be sure, it was not the only company that diversified successfully during the period in question; there were others that did notably well, too. But there were also numerous diversification failures among companies in the communications and related industries, as a brief perusal of *Forbes, Business Week,* and corporate annual reports will show. The company never seemed in real danger of joining this list.

Varieties of Strength

The cornerstone of the inside-out approach is the key abilities, strengths, and aptitudes of an organization. In some cases, as already indicated, these may prove to be in the marketing, engineering, or financial departments. In other cases the key might be an unusual forecasting talent, or a unique manufacturing capability. Then again it might be simply location, as when a company, store, or college finds it has the most advantageous spot in an area from which to serve many people. Or it might be a set of patents, or a happenstance of size or reputation, or possession of unique physical facilities.

The railroads are a case in point. Up until the early 1960's, these carriers were the classic example in the marketing literature of an industry that had thought of itself too narrowly, without regard for changing trends in the market and in competition, and which therefore was becoming defunct. However serious their "marketing myopia" was, they did retain one precious and unique asset: positions, rights, and facilities which nobody else could duplicate and which *could* be made more useful to people in the manner originally intended. New York Central head Alfred E. Perlman was one of the men who saw this. When he took over the Central in 1954, the company was actually investigating bankruptcy as a solution to its problems. ("My first day on the job I was told that we had $6 million in the bank and a $35 million payroll to meet.") Nevertheless, the Central—and only the Central—had the rights, track, and rolling stock to move freight cars between specified cities. Perlman bent all his efforts on developing this asset. At the same time that he cut costs as a defensive move, he began pouring every cent he could find into new freight cars, better railroad yards, better communications, and other equipment. Gradually the Central's fortunes began improving. By its own actions, the company began bringing apparently dead markets to life.

Although the kinds of strengths important in inside-out analysis can vary greatly, they must meet two requirements. They must (1) influence, and seem likely to continue to influence, the organization's fortunes in a vital way and (2) be within the realm of management's power to preserve, refine, improve, and/or extend. (A period of unusually low accident rates, for instance, would not be a strength for a casualty insurance firm, since it cannot control the temporary factors causing the low rates.)

Important Assumptions

Turning now to more theoretical aspects of the inside-out approach, let us examine some of the key assumptions used.

One very important idea concerns marketing power. Inside-outers assume that they have a certain measure of influence over the market—that up to a point they can mold it by their own actions. "Often you can create a market *by what you do*," they say. The very act of making and promoting a new product or service may awaken desires that were not formerly noticeable. I know of a prosperous electronics firm, for instance, which looked long and hard at some of its strategic choices in a rapidly changing industry. A few years ago its executives were debating whether or not it should go into the miniaturization business. One man felt strongly that it should, even though there were many question marks still around sales prospects. "We develop a product, then find a need for it," he said. "Most successful things are like that around here." In short, he felt that, given a smart engineering advance, management could create a market where none existed before.

A second basic assumption is that differences in ability between competing organizations are enormously important—more so, often, than differences in the markets served. (In education and government, the same assumption would hold for colleges and agencies serving sectors of public needs.) Companies that look alike to the outside observer may differ as significantly in outlook and capability as brothers with the same facial and body characteristics. Here I can do no better than quote from Peter Drucker. Referring to three well-known chemical firms, he states:

All three companies have done well over the years. To the outsider they look much alike. They all have big research centers, big plants, sales organizations, and so on. They all work in the same lines of chemistry. They are about equal in capital investment and in sales. They all show about the same substantial returns on investment. But one company always does well if it can bring a product or product line into the consumer market. The second company is outstanding in its ability to develop new chemical specialties for the industrial user. Again and again it has tried to break into the consumer market; and it has failed in the attempt again and again. The third company is not doing particularly well in either the consumer or the industrial market. Its return on sales is quite low compared to the other two. But it has tremendous income from licensing developments, coming out of its research, to other chemical companies—developments which apparently the company itself does not know how to turn into successful products and profitable sales.

The first and the third company are obviously strong in original research. The second one says of itself—and only half in jest—"We haven't had one original idea in the last twenty years." But it has amazing ability to see the potentials of commercial development in somebody else's half-formulated idea or in a laboratory curiosity; to acquire the rights to the idea; and to convert it into salable chemical specialties for industrial use.

Each of the three companies has come to understand what it can do and what it cannot do. Each sets its goals and measures its performance in terms of its specific knowledge: the first in terms of success in the consumer market; the second in terms of the new successful chemical specialties it develops; the third in terms of the ratio of license fees received to research budget.[3]

Third, inside-out places more emphasis on what an organization has proved itself able to do than on opportunities per se or on stated management creeds and desires. What those who follow the approach seem to be saying, in effect, is this: "Never mind what we think it would be nice to do well, when we get to wishing. Never mind even what the biggest market opportunities are for somebody who knows how to take them. Let's look at what we do every day, and let's see from that what we're really good at. Let's be objective and factual about this, as analytical as we possibly can be."

Conflict with Marketing?

Though the inside-out approach to goal setting does not reject the marketing viewpoint, but only tends to postpone it in the goal-setting process, marketing people may be disturbed by it. At first blush it may appear to them that marketing is treated as a "second team" activity. Is this really the case? I do not think so.

If a strong marketing orientation happens to be the real strength of the organization, that is indeed the correct place to begin thinking and discussions. However, only a minority of organizations can have marketing talents that are well above average.

There is also a kind of marketing judgment that is built into appraisals of organizational ability in an inside-out analysis. The very fact that an organization has demonstrated superiority in a certain way implies that the market has accepted the ability or resources accounting for that superiority. If the record shows, let us say, that your organization has consistently succeeded in

[3] Peter Drucker, *Managing for Results* (New York: Harper & Row, 1964), pp. 115–116.

training salesmen well for conventional, established, well-known lines of insurance (as opposed to the newer "growth" lines), then you can infer that the market likes and needs this kind of effort. Similarly, if your analysis of organizational performance shows you always have done best when you have invested heavily in basic research efforts and have bet on break-through products in your strategy instead of commercialization of already-developed notions, then you can infer that the market likes and needs what you produce in this way. If the market had not liked it, the record would not show superiority, for superiority is measured in terms of earnings performance.

Ever-Present Dangers

On the liability side, the first and perhaps most sobering possibility is that inside-out will play into the hands of those who want their departments and divisions to keep doing the same old things they have always done, not because of facts and analysis, but because it is the easiest, most comfortable course. There are some careful observers in the business world today who feel that planning has at times been subverted into a tool for preserving the status quo. We do not know whether or not this has been done under the auspices of an inside-out brand of reasoning; however, it *could* be distorted into a kind of protective umbrella for status quo seekers. They might point to cases of companies that have concentrated successfully on narrow, traditional product lines by virtue of inside-out planning. They might equate the inside-out approach with such cases, arguing that inside-out always says, in effect, "Shoemaker, stick to thy last." In so interpreting the philosophy they would, of course, be in error.

The most eloquent critique of status quo planning I know of has been made by John B. McKitterick. His remarks illuminate the danger of letting inside-out or any other philosophy be distorted into a carte blanche justification of sticking with traditional products, processes, policies, and strategies:

Our planning has tended to become a mere administrative process of endless criteria, and the creative quality of the alternatives examined is scarcely worthy of the sterile perfection of the decision system applied. As a result, imaginative ideas entailing some real element of uncertainty tend to be cast aside in preference for safe trivia. Yet, as we have seen, the profit rewards from endlessly doing old things more efficiently also are trivial. Indeed, the obvious which is quickly imitated by competition may turn out to be a far more risky investment than some unique and original conception. It certainly is ironic that the very efficiency of the bureaucratic process within our businesses tends to create an atmosphere that is highly toxic to originality and risk-taking.[4]

Other concepts of goal setting—the strategic missions approach popularized by Secretary of Defense Robert McNamara, for instance, or possibly even the outside-in approach—might be distorted in the same way. What makes inside-out more vulnerable than other concepts is that it is evolutionary in nature rather than revolutionary. While it may lead to radically different markets, products, and services, it leads in such directions only if warranted by the development of currently existing abilities and resources. The latter are always the key consideration. In this sense, inside-out is a conservative philosophy, and this characteristic, if misunderstood or exaggerated, may cause trouble. Evolution is misconstrued as gradualism; gradualism is misconstrued as specialization. In the words of Wroe Alderson:

One tendency that has appeared many times both in biological and cultural evolution is for specialization in a given direction to lead progressively to still further specialization. In the biological field this tendency sometimes gets out of hand, specialization proceeding far beyond any functional value. An illustrative case is that of a species of elk whose horns finally grew so large that they apparently contributed to the extinction of the species. The trilobite and some other fossils are believed to represent the dead end of specialization in certain evolutionary lines.

[4] See David W. Ewing, editor, *Long-Range Planning for Management* (New York: Harper & Row, 1964), p. 75.

Something like this appears to happen frequently with products and ways of living although the mechanisms involved are obviously quite different. Thus, in the manufacture of automobiles the momentum of specialization has been exhibited in such matters as increasing horsepower and the profusion of chrome fittings. The competitive principle appears to be that if a certain feature will attract customers then giving them more of the same will have even greater attraction. . . .

Some students of the automobile industry feel that the competitive value of step-by-step change is about to become exhausted and that the time for truly radical innovation is approaching. [5]

A second shortcoming of the inside-out approach is that the presently held abilities and resources which it focuses on may become out of date, or become less potent for some reason in future situations. A leading textile company followed a kind of inside-out reasoning to lay out an ambitious marketing program for certain piece goods. Using the pattern of some successful small campaigns in the past, it formulated a major program of promotion through magazines, television, radio, and other media. Its reasoning was that its salespeople had previously demonstrated a particular kind of ability to entice the consumer and that if it invested more heavily in this ability, it would produce correspondingly good results in the future.

The campaign was a miserable failure. During an agonizing period of post mortems, one executive summed up the trouble as follows: "Basically we went wrong because we tried to make something grow that just didn't want to grow. We tried to lift ourselves up by our boot straps; we were more or less intoxicated with three or four consecutive years of success with this type of promotion. We said, 'Gee, if we did that much only half trying, what could we do if we really tried?' " The reasoning had seemed irrefutable at the time, but as he and other managers had come to realize, the particular abilities that made the first small cam-

[5] See Robert M. Kaplan, editor, *The Marketing Concept in Action* (Chicago: American Marketing Association, 1964), p. 150.

paigns successful were of limited value—good on a small scale but not on a large one.

One can imagine other kinds of example. Suppose that the real talents of a welfare agency lie in rescuing and retraining alcoholics—and that a sure cure for alcoholism is found. No amount or quality of investment in the organization's unique talent will pay off.

Still, there are things management can do to reduce the threat. For example, it can guard against defining the organization's distinctive proficiency too narrowly. A leather supplier's competence may seem to be outmoded by the arrival of Corfam and other synthetic substitutes for leather; beneath the organization's facility with leather products, however, there may lie more basic abilities which are by no means obsolete. Again, management can subject its inside-out conclusions to a rigorous marketing forecast at some stage in the goal-setting process. A strategy based on the development of key abilities can be regarded as no more than tentative until marketing estimates are reviewed. "Distinctive competence," as one strategist has noted, "is not something to be defined and forgotten, but a subject for continuing analysis and investment."[6]

A third danger is that inside-out will inhibit executives from considering radical leaps and changes—the visionary, far-out ones that succeed despite every possible objection and criticism simply because they are so brilliantly conceived or have so much capacity to stir enthusiasm. "Don't be afraid to take a big step if one is indicated," David Lloyd George once said. "You can't cross a chasm in two small jumps."

A fourth danger has to do with the economics of a situation. No matter how clearly a certain strategy may seem to be dictated by a given organization strength or resource, there is always the possibility that the realities of competition or temporary

---

[6] Seymour Tilles, "Strategies for Allocating Funds," *Harvard Business Review*, January–February, 1966, p. 79.

economic circumstances may make the strategy impractical, at least for the time being. For instance, as Edmund P. Learned and his associates note, "A small rubber company in an industry led by U.S. Rubber, Goodyear, Goodrich, and Firestone, will not, under the economic condition of overcapacity, elect to provide the automobile business with original tires for new cars."[7] Even a large and well-financed corporation will want to take a hard look at competitive circumstances. Campbell Soup, which a *Fortune* writer aptly described as "Top Tomato" in its business, tried once to break into the market for catsup. Despite Campbell Soup's eminent qualifications for such a venture, it failed, presumably because the market just could not take another large producer.

Another example is provided by Riegel Paper Corporation. In early 1966 this shrewdly managed company was contemplating the economic future of its industry. It felt that competitors were scheduling new pulp capacity at a frightening rate. Riegel's abilities made it a logical candidate for keeping well invested in pulp capacity, and management felt that the *long-run* prospects in this end of the business were good. But in the interim it felt that it would make a better profit showing if it concentrated on semi-finished and finished products, which it was also successful at making. It planned, therefore, to do more spending on paper machines in the immediate future than it would have done otherwise—more than presumably would have been dictated by a purely inside-out strategy.

As the Riegel Paper example suggests, this fourth danger of inside-out can be readily contained. It can be contained in much the same way that the second danger can be: by considering any inside-out decision tentative until a careful economic analysis is made. Is the goal set by inside-out methods reasonable in view of various economic and market factors which the organization must contend with? If it is not, then alternatives should be examined.

[7] *Business Policy: Text and Cases* (Homewood, Ill.: Richard D. Irwin, 1965), p. 173.

They may be drastic departures from inside-out or, as in the Riegel case, simply temporary changes in emphasis.

Choosing the Most Rewarding Goal

Once management has in mind clear judgments about the main talents and abilities of the organization, it is ready to proceed with the following steps:

1. "Beefing up" the vital abilities. What further strengthening would result if management gave the fullest possible support to the abilities that seem most important?

2. Examining the strategic moves that could be made if this strengthening were accomplished. What might be done if new strengths or resources were added?

3. Choosing from these possibilities the one or ones that look best for the organization from a marketing (or, in the case of education or government, from a service) point of view. On the basis of forecasts and insights into demand, which objectives would seem to promise the greatest return?

These steps complete the inside-out approach to setting strategic goals. They are not taken in a neat hop-skip-and-jump sequence, but tend to overlap and intermingle. (If the outside-in approach is followed, the basic order is different. Market analysis comes first; then the investigation of strengths and ways of developing strengths so that the best possible choice of goals is made. However, for convenience of exposition in this chapter we shall assume use of the inside-out method.)

One thing must be emphasized: The inside-out approach to goal setting is not necessarily "for headquarters only." *It is equally useful in departments and divisions of an organization.* To be sure, broad elections of goals may already have been made for them by headquarters. A division may be committed, before its managers can go ahead with their own plans, to concentrating on low-risk products, or the manufacturing department may be already committed to producing certain lines of equipment, or the personnel department may be already committed to recruiting and training a definite number of people for specified types of work. In cases like this, the managers eliminate from their consideration those goals inconsistent with the over-all strategy of the corporation, university, or agency. They work within the range of electives that *are* permissible (even if it is only one), identifying the abilities that count most toward success, judging how these abilities might be built up, and comparing alternatives thus made possible which are consistent with the corporate strategy. For example:

- The broad corporate strategy of the ABC Gas Company may call for each local company to develop a certain quota of gas appliance sales. The XYZ company, one of the locals, may have a very poor record of merchandising gas appliances, and, if it had its way, might choose to stay out of this part of the business completely and concentrate on gas service only. But since it is committed by headquarters to appliance marketing, it will begin with those of its abilities which have most to do with success in this line and then proceed with the steps indicated. The particular approach to the appliance marketing it chooses—the kind of marketing technique it emphasizes—will be chosen on this basis.
- Suppose the ABC Company strategy calls for *no* appliance sales emphasis in any local company, but the XYZ local has especially *great* potential for appliance marketing? Then just the opposite happens: XYZ management eliminates this possible goal from consideration and does not go into developing its merchandising strength for appliance selling.
- For a simple example from nonprofit organizations, take *Harvard Business Review*. If we were to assess the various abilities this organization has demonstrated and look at the possibilities for strengthening the most potent ones, we might find that HBR would do well to plan to diversify, let us say, into the commercial book-club business. But HBR is an edu-

cational arm of the Harvard Business School, and moving into commercial book-club operations would not be consistent with the School's broad aims of educating managers. But the abilities just mentioned might, if suitably developed, lead to new objectives that *would* be appropriate for a Harvard publication.

With these general considerations in mind, let us turn to the first two steps just listed. How, exactly, does management begin to proceed from organizational self-appraisal to the choice of a goal or goals?

1. Strengthening Present Abilities

In most cases, managers should be able to find a good variety of ways of building up a key talent or strength. The possibilities may range from special techniques to fairly general types of approaches. The following questions are meant to suggest a few of these possibilities.

Can technical talents be enriched? Several years ago an electronics company producing analog computers was investigating the advisability of going into microelectronic circuits. This prospect had opened up because of the excellent engineering talents developed by the company—talents which had already moved it part of the way into solid-state designs employing microminiaturization. In looking at the possibilities of beefing up these talents, managers considered such moves as taking on production development work for a defense laboratory and encouraging company engineers to continue going about the industry (perhaps even more so than in the past) asking questions, acquiring knowledge, and experimenting with new ideas on a pilot scale.

Can the efforts of key people be better directed? Another example of a company with a strong engineering talent is cited by Peter Drucker. The company prided itself on a department of several hundred expensive top-flight engineers. Although they worked hard, they were not working effectively; they were spending a great deal of time on "interesting" problems which did not greatly affect the fortunes of the company.[8] By focusing more of these talents on the most lucrative customers and marketing opportunities, management could have greatly increased its goals for sales volume and profits (and perhaps found resources for diversification at the same time).

What about better methods and tactics? Frequently divisions and departments of companies find they can get far more mileage from key people by training them to use better methods and strategies. To illustrate, an industrial marketer may discover that it can greatly increase the effectiveness of its salesmen in launching new products by replanning call schedules. If field sales engineers approach potential customers on several levels, calling on production personnel and financial executives in the prospect companies as well as on purchasing agents, they may be able to ring up many more successes.[9]

Would organizational changes increase a key strength? In the case of N. V. Philips Gloeilampenfabrieken, the great Dutch-based electronics firm, a vital organizational ability is reinforced by a tailor-made managerial pattern. Although Philips spends millions on research each year, it is usually not the first to launch a new product on the market. It waits until the market shows signs of fast growth and then moves in. Its managers and technical people have demonstrated real ability to play this game, over the years, and the company's excellent market standing in many product lines attests to that fact.

However, such an ability calls for a flexible corporate organization, one that can move swiftly and efficiently when just the right time comes. Management saw that there were systematic ways of expanding this ability. One was to develop an intricate two-di-

---

[8] Peter F. Drucker, "Managing for Business Effectiveness," *Harvard Business Review*, May–June, 1963, p. 55.

[9] See E. Raymond Corey, *Industrial Marketing* (Englewood Cliffs, N.J.: Prentice-Hall, 1962), pp. 248–262, 453–454.

mensional structure, with twin-headed leadership of each division. A division is run jointly by a "commercial" man and a "technical" man, both accountable for division results. The two managers act as a check on each other—guarding against overzealousness and also overcautiousness. In the opinion of many managers, the system has had much to do with Philips' superb growth in a long series of world markets and industries.[10]

Can personal values be made more reinforcing? In their study of managerial values (see Chapter 6), William D. Guth and Renato Tagiuri cite the case of a company whose president was pondering a choice of strategies. His decision was complicated by the fact that one of his vice-presidents was a businessman-scientist who placed a high value on research leadership, another vice-president emphasized profitability and workaday efficiency, and another felt somewhat hostile to the prospects of company growth.

Such value heterogeneity can cripple operations (although it did not in the aforementioned case because of the president's discernment and wisdom). Management does not need to succumb to "group-think" and conformism to seek a mixture of values that will be dynamic rather than paralyzing—a balance that will be creative and mutually reinforcing rather than destructive of vigorous leadership.

A warning. It is tempting to confuse abilities with products and services because products and services are simpler, more tangible, more immediate. Also, of course, they tend to be identified with certain groups and individuals in an organization. Yet present products and services are the source of today's rewards only, not necessarily tomorrow's. Thinking in terms of products rather than core abilities may lead directly to "marketing myopia," which is fatal to creative planning.

I know one company that does a superb job of seeking out the critical operating characteristics of each major product—the

[10] *International Management,* March, 1965, pp. 17–20.

characteristics which, if improved a little, could help sales and profits most. When the characteristics are pinpointed, they become the focus of applied research. This is a fine and praiseworthy effort, but not the kind of talent development needed for inside-out planning. Because it is useful and easily explained, the approach mentioned (or ones like it) will be "in the air" a large part of the time wherever planning work is attempted. One of the most important jobs of the inside-out planner, therefore, is educating the organization to the subtle differences between strengthening vital talents and strengthening critical product or service characteristics.

2. Identifying Possible Moves

With a good understanding of important organizational abilities and of how much they can be developed further, management can look around at strategic goals which could be established realistically. Concentrating on ability development rather than product development, executives are less likely to fall into the trap of defining the future by what has been done in the past, or of imitating the diversification strategies of industry leaders, or of applying textbook solutions to their problems. In short, the idea is to explore, to be imaginative, to be inquiring. Perhaps later investigation (the third-step marketing appraisal) will show that the best bet is to "stay put" and seek to do an ever-improving job of it. But we want to be in the position of knowing what we really can do well before eliminating any options.

This is the kind of thinking that helped lead the aerospace companies to decide, sometime around 1963 and 1964, that their unique abilities could be applied profitably to shipbuilding. Litton Industries saw that it had the know-how to make money on automated ships, Boeing recognized its capabilities to build hydrofoil submarine chasers for the U.S. Navy, Bell Aerosystems saw the possibilities of diversifying into hovercraft (which it did with the help of a license from Great Britain's Saunders-Roe

Aircraft), and similar moves were envisioned by a number of other aerospace firms. Today, aerospace companies are also venturing into rail transportation.

Special measures to add strength. Sometimes, when possible moves are imagined in this manner, management will become interested in an "almost possible" objective. It will be one which the organization is not equipped to take on right away but could undertake if it added a strength or resource not currently possessed. For example, a number of United States companies decided in the early 1960's that they had technological, service, and production know-hows that were highly salable in Europe. But they needed local distribution systems and good will to do the job, and it would take years to create such resources if they started from scratch. So they purchased companies in Europe which had the missing requirements, thus completing quickly the "profile" of talents that happened to be needed.

Sometimes, too, an analysis of strategic possibilities will point to the desirability of a *defensive* move in order to *protect* the organization's strengths. For instance, an electronics company had a unique ability in circuit design. As its executives looked at trends in their industry, a few years ago, they foresaw that more and more manufacturers of microelectronic circuits—the firms that would be potential customers—would be getting into circuit design work, too. If these customers developed such a capability, would they not be able to copy the company's designs and market them? In other words, might not working with these firms lead to the company's losing its unique capability in design and eventually its market? This possibility led some executives to argue that the company should plan to move into the manufacture of microelectronic circuits as well as their design.

Divestment of unprofitable operations is another example of a defensive move, since it eliminates drains on the strengths of the company.

The Precious Task of Appraisal

6

A top executive of an aggressive petrochemical corporation was asked how his company made up its mind about what it could and could not do and how rapidly it could take action. He answered, "An awful lot depends on your ability to look at yourself, at your company strengths and deficiencies realistically. It is a precious task in long-range planning."

All around the world, where planning has been done, and through all the ages, the "precious task" of organizational self-appraisal has held the secret, in one case after another, to whether or not strategic goals have been set soundly. The realistic, perceptive appraisal has saved from disaster many a program which was not otherwise well designed. And lack of a good appraisal has led to catastrophe many another program which was otherwise designed to perfection.

Yet this precious task of appraisal has received relatively little attention in the literature of planning. Thumbing through different books and articles, you can find many mentions of the importance of "strengths and weaknesses," "controlling factors," "key abilities," and similarly worded items. But try to find any extended discussion of such items, and especially of what they mean and how they are found, and you will be frustrated. There is a fairly complete blackout on the art of self-appraisal.

What makes this blackout all the more surprising is that the task is "precious" regardless of an organization's planning philosophy. Whether it is outside-in, inside-out, or some other variety, sound goals depend on sound self-appraisals. An executive team can gorge itself on facts about different market opportunities, but if it lacks a realistic idea of the organization's capabilities, it cannot digest the facts properly.

Abilities to Look For

"Individual and unsupported flashes of strength," states one team of authorities, "are not as dependable as the gradually accumulated product- and market-related fruits of experience."[1] Experienced planners will find little fault with this statement. It is the proved, demonstrated, relatively lasting qualities that you want to size up, not the more transient abilities that may fade from the picture even before a plan comes to be implemented. But these qualities are not general ones like faith, hope, and charity; they are talents peculiar to specific organizations and situations, and in a sizable organization they may vary widely from operation to operation.

William C. Treuhaft, president of Tremco Manufacturing Company, once pointed out that in his maintenance products division the crucial role was played by the number of effective sales personnel in the field; hence the key planning task was to make sure good recruiting, training, and supervisory programs were maintained. But in other divisions of the company, Treuhaft pointed out, the situation was different. In several, new products were the master key to growth and profitability. In them, it was the division's ability to produce a new model, new application, or

[1] Edmund P. Learned, C. Roland Christensen, Kenneth R. Andrews, and William D. Guth, *Business Policy: Text and Cases* (Homewood, Ill.: Richard D. Irwin, 1965), p. 179.

new product line which, more than anything else, told the story.

Perhaps most important in organizational appraisal is focusing on *abilities* rather than aspirations, on *strengths* rather than status, on *aptitudes* and *values* rather than verbalizations. Managers are urged by some analysts to dwell on such matters as whether or not they have thoroughly trained marketing organizations, a good balance of scientists in research, capacity for the level of volume that has been forecast, a strong financial position, and so on. To the thoughtful executive, such advice must seem to miss the main point. A strong financial position is always useful, but it may or may not be vital; a good balance of scientists is advantageous, but it may or may not be essential to research success; the right amount of production capacity is always economic, but it may or may not be a high-priority factor in planning ahead. Nothing can answer such questions for an executive except the record of his own organization. Always it is what his organization can *do* best that really counts—and especially, what it can do in relation to the specific strategic goals it is considering.

With these general observations in mind, let us examine different kinds of strengths to look for.

Easily Recognized Functional Abilities

Sometimes an organization's key ability can be defined in terms like quality purchasing, mass distribution, or clever merchandising. For instance, you may hear managers in the food business say that A&P's real strength is not its size, image, advertising, or costs—that in these respects it cannot do anything its competitors cannot do. Where A&P has a real edge on many other stores, these managers say, is in the shrewdness of its buyers. It has an army of men and women who can buy peas, tomatoes, butter, cheese, meat, milk, and other items with an eye for quality and salability that few food buyers possess. In the trade, some of these buyers are known by name, and more than once one has been called "the best in the country."

In planning what A&P can do in the future, it is therefore especially important to solve problems that affect this buying function and to create programs that will make it stronger and more useful to the company (assuming, of course, that buying is expected to remain a vital factor in the trade). What management thinks it can accomplish in these respects is the vital variable in its strategic planning. (Other activities will need much attention, too, as we shall see in a later chapter, but they play a supporting role rather than a commanding one.)

Go on to Celanese Corporation, however, and you will hear a different account. Here is a company which possesses a marvelous ability to glamorize and sell a textile product. It is said that when Celanese came out with Arnel, for example, it had a fiber which competitors could match with similar fibers. But with its deft marketing touch, Celanese could do what they could not, and sales of Arnel boomed. Celanese's marketing skill was so great, in fact, that it could count on doing better if it depended more on its own "feel" for customer preferences and dealt with the customer himself if possible rather than if it analyzed information from the garment manufacturers to whom it sold. "Our manufacturing customers tell us what *they* want," President Harold Blancke told a reporter, "not what their customers want. We're asked to meet specifications, not to fill consumer needs."[2]

In a case like this, the wise management emphasizes recruiting, training, and supervising shrewd marketers and developing excellent marketing programs. As it does this, it will need to build up the supporting operations, too, for the marketers cannot "do it alone." But they are the vital variable, and strategic thinking must be predicted on their expected future potential.

Underlying Talents

Often the abilities that count most for planning are not on the surface at all. They are on no organization chart, no list of func-

[2] *Forbes,* July 15, 1964, p. 37.

tions. Rather, they are talents that run across and through various operations and activities. Although subtle, they are unmistakably in evidence and have a pervasive influence on performance. They can be developed (or damaged) just as surely and systematically as can any functional ability.

Gordon Conrad of Arthur D. Little, Inc., suggests defining a "basic profile" of the unique talents and aptitudes which affect performance. What he recognizes is that in most cases there is not one but a series of key abilities and that the combination of them is likely to be more important than any one or two individually. In addition, he recognizes that in a company of any size the core talents will be exercised not by one man but by a group of people, with the implication that a kind of momentum will have been achieved which will survive the departure of any one or two individuals.

Illustrating his thesis, Conrad suggests that a close look at the basic profile of a railroad might reveal such strengths as (to mention just a few):

1. Ability to negotiate and manipulate complex rate schedules with federal agencies.

2. Experience in living under the close scrutiny of regulatory agencies.

3. Know-how in inducing industries to locate and develop in new regions.

4. Skill at complex scheduling of interrelated operations.

While not necessarily unique when taken separately, Conrad points out, such abilities might add up to a profile unlike that of other companies. If management were planning diversification, the profile might suggest moving into the electric utility business.

Turning to another example, Conrad puts the following talents in the profile of a distiller and national marketer of whiskies:

1. Sophistication in natural commodity trading.

2. Knowledge of complex warehousing procedures.

3. Ability in dealing with state government agencies.
4. Marketing experience at both the wholesale and retail levels.
5. Advertising know-how.

Such a profile, he concludes, might well justify the distiller's moving (if it sought to diversify) into the building products industry, where it would be trading in lumber or its by-products instead of grain, dealing again with state political groups, and marketing still at the wholesale and retail levels in combination.[3]

Basic Values, Attitudes, and Aptitudes

One of the most tragic illusions in planning is that "hard facts" alone can determine what goals and courses of action should be taken. Again and again we hear statements such as "The company's peculiar strengths and weaknesses determine its optimum strategy." This is nonsense. To begin with, of course, it is people who decide strategy, not an analysis. Second, since people's interpretations of information are influenced heavily by their values and attitudes, these latter should be taken prominently into account. How much value is attached to profitability as opposed to security? How much weight is put on being "first" rather than "safest"? How much interest is there in risk taking? And so forth.

A group of executives at the Harvard Business School Advanced Management Program once told about a company that undertook to develop an exciting new product. The managers and engineers in the research and development department strongly supported the venture, and they sold top management on backing it to the tune of $4 million, four years of research work, and the allocation of considerable technical talent to the job. When the time came to put the new product on the market for testing and large-scale distribution, the research men learned to their dismay

[3] Gordon R. Conrad, "Unexplored Assets for Diversification," *Harvard Business Review*, September–October, 1963, pp. 71, 73.

that the company was not ready to go ahead with these tasks. There had been little or no thinking about market research, distribution methods, and all the other supporting activities that were necessary to commercialize the product once it came out of the laboratory. All momentum on the project was lost, the company's time advantage over competitors disappeared, and when a competitor came on the market with a similar product, top management wrote the venture off completely. While it had given lip service to the new idea, it was not really prepared to back it to the hilt. The interest in taking risks with really new products was nowhere near as strong at the top of the company as it was in the R & D department.

This is a fine example of the importance of values in strategic planning. Values are not as specific as bricks, mortar, staff size, and distribution channels, but they can be a good deal more influential in making planning work. Without a good appraisal or "feeling" for the predominant values in its thinking, management cannot be well prepared to set major goals and courses of action.

If goals are tailored reasonably well to the predominant values in an organization, values can then truly be called a resource. Risk-taking values greatly increase the chances that risky goals will be achieved as hoped; control values increase the chance that orderly progress toward named goals will be achieved when that is the plan; and so on. It is only when values are inconsistent with the corporate strategy that they become liabilities—and, in many cases, debilitating liabilities—to the whole program.

Other Strengths

The resources just described do not exhaust the list, although they account for most of it. For instance, the crucial strength on which to base plans might be simply a geographical position: an especially good corner of town for a retail store to be located, let us say, or a commanding military position like the Rock of Gibraltar. In either case, the ambition and magnitude of the planned goal would hinge more on what could be done to exploit the advantages of the position than on anything else.

Perhaps we are doing little more than taking an old adage, "Know thyself," and dressing it up for an executive board meeting. If so, we can justify giving so much attention to this ancient insight by noting the dangers of forgetting it. Some wise observations on this score have been made by Adrian J. Grossman of General Electric Company:

> Many an on-going business fails in its planning to utilize or to exploit its greatest strength—*itself*. It is apt (1) to accumulate an abundance of data with respect to its markets, its competitors and even its resources, (2) to display this evidence whenever a member of the board inquires as to the status of its planning or one of its professional planners writes a learned paper, and (3) to file the reports in multi-colored splendor.
>
> I hold that such use of planning efforts can be traced either to failure to establish an identity differentiating the business, and to use this identity as a focus to pinpoint markets, competitors and resources in terms relevant to the pivotal entrepreneurial decisions currently needed; or to reliance on an identity—perhaps only dimly seen—appropriate to the past but not consonant with the reality of the present.
>
> So characterized, a business is likely (1) to be unduly concerned with what its competitors are doing or plan to do, (2) to respond vigorously to such actions, more often than not by imitating, and (3) to evaluate itself not on the extent to which it has realized its potential as much as on its competitive ranking.[4]

Making the Appraisal

"How do you *make* a good appraisal for planning purposes?" the manager asks. "In our organization we know we should make the most of our strengths when we map out a strategy. We've

---

[4] "Inner-Directedness in Planning," in E. Kirby Warren, editor, *Proceedings of the Seventh Annual Symposium on Planning*, May, 1964 (Pleasantville, N.Y.: The Institute of Management Sciences, 1965).

known that for a long time. What we want to know is this: What's
the secret of finding out what our real strengths *are?* How come
we can't hit the answer almost every time, as that company a
couple of blocks away does? Are appraisals for planning different
from other appraisals?"

Many managers are ready to agree that the effort to appraise
an organization's talents is valuable and worth while. The attempt
alone is generally productive. But some attempts lead to a larger
pay-off for planning than do others. Why? What can we learn
in this respect from managerial experience in business, government, and education?

Organizational appraisal is not a task that can be formularized
—at least, for purposes of setting up strategic goals. The reason
is that such an appraisal is not simply a valuation of resources
as of the moment but a valuation for a period of time extending
into the future. And one of the forces influencing the future
growth or retardation of those resources is management itself.
Hence management, when it makes an appraisal for planning, is
appraising not employees and facilities alone but employees and
facilities *in combination with* itself, in particular with its skill
and desire to direct them during the planning period.

Consider a buyer of industrial property. The price he is willing
to pay reflects not simply the market value of the land, buildings,
and equipment but also their value to him as he thinks he can
use them. The kind of appraisal he makes, therefore, is similar to
an organizational appraisal for strategic planning. On the other
hand, the kind of appraisal made by the seller or his broker
would not be similar. Their estimate reflects only what they believe a buyer will pay them now. For another analogy, take trad,
ing of players in professional football. What a team will offer
for a player owned by another team reflects his record to date
and the head office's best guess as to how well the man will fit
in with present and planned personnel, anticipated changes in
coaching and playing tactics, and so forth. This kind of estimate,
too, is similar to that made in planning.

Veridical Perception

Of three general methods of making organizational appraisals, the one most commonly favored is what businessman-writer Harry Schrage calls the "veridical" approach. The word "veridical," as used here, implies that the manager observes pertinent conditions directly, personally, immediately, factually, accurately. It implies seeing, feeling, sensing, being there—these qualities as opposed to judging on the basis of hearsay, wish, or rules of thumb borrowed from others. The veridical approach combines two views in the same estimate; the eyes that look outward at the organization's personnel and facilities are the same eyes that look inward at management's intentions and desires for the future.

What characterizes veridical perception in everyday practice? When Schrage interviewed the heads of new companies with technologically advanced products and processes, he ran into two different types of thinking.[5] For example, he would ask for the executive's opinion about the expected future sales volume of a new product and receive the following kind of answer:

I am convinced it will increase with time. I have always developed absolutely the finest in this line of equipment. The trouble is that each time I get going with a particular design, they (government) change their minds and decide they want something else. This time I'm sure, though, because I have a good amount of back-orders on hand.

The following typifies a second, quite different kind of answer to the same question in another company:

I have asked most of my customers what their anticipated volume will be in the foreseeable future. Their replies indicate that I can

[5] "The R & D Entrepreneur: Personality and Profitability," a thesis for the Alfred P. Sloan School of Management, Massachusetts Institute of Technology, June, 1965. Also see the same author's article, "The R & D Entrepreneur: Profile of Success," *Harvard Business Review*, November–December, 1965, p. 56.

expect the current level of demand to continue for at least the next year.

The second answer, Schrage points out, illustrates the veridical approach: the executive appears to have actually sought out information from his customers. But the first answer does not: the executive here seems to avoid such information. Schrage illustrates further with contrasting answers from the same two men to a question concerning whether or not customers seemed satisfied with a particular product:

Nonveridical: "You bet they are. They wouldn't be buying from me if they weren't. Besides, every time a customer re-orders, you know he is satisfied."

Veridical: "The response is mixed but improving. Our sales representatives or I always visit our customers periodically: not to land orders but to find out what complaints they have, if any. Our deliveries are still a little slow to some accounts, but we haven't had a major complaint on quality for over six months."

Correlating his interview data with data on the success of the different companies he studied, Schrage finds that the veridical approach commonly characterizes firms with improving profits and market positions, while the nonveridical approach characterizes firms in trouble. Editorializing on this finding, he states:

The "losers" either "know" the answers without looking or decide that it is useless to try to find out. Their thoughts seem to revolve about their inventions. They have little concern for what goes on out there [the market], filling this void with their own preconceived notions.

The "winners," on the other hand, appear to admit that they don't know enough and spend much time looking for the answers in the marketplace. They sound as if they have managed to transfer some of their scientific curiosity to business matters.

Significantly, the same contrasts appear in Schrage's study when he asks entrepreneurs about employee morale. Here are examples of two kinds of answer to a question concerning whether morale in the shop is good:

Nonveridical: "Morale in my company is excellent. We recently landed a number of contracts and people always feel good when there is plenty of work ahead. I have decided that engineers and scientists usually become unhappy when they're not doing a good job. Then they just get depressed and leave."

Veridical #1: "My office is located so that every man who comes in or goes out of the building passes by my door, and the door is always open. They know they are welcome to come in and tell me their troubles. I know this takes much of my personal time, but it pays off."

Veridical #2: "In some departments it's better than in others. When my company was small, I used to spend much time with the people in the shop. Now I instruct my supervisors to stay close to their people and to find out whenever something bothers them. Then there are some of the older employees who have been with us from the start. They frequently come to see me at my office and tell me what is going on."

Executives who are skilled at appraising their organizations' talents and resources can attest to the importance of veridical perception. Naturally it would be an error to suppose that every manager who uses it will guess right; and it would also be an error to suppose that every manager who does not use it guesses wrong. Yet most men who have proven themselves astute at sizing up strengths and weaknesses would agree without qualification, I believe, that veridical perception is one of their two or three most important "secrets."

Significance for Planning. Now, what is the importance of all this for planning? First and most obvious, an accurate appraisal of current resources makes a better starting point for a program than does an inaccurate or vague appraisal. Second, veridical perception will ordinarily give the manager a better "feel" or "sixth sense" for what can and cannot be done in the future—

for what can be accomplished with the human abilities and physical resources he sees and studies and under the direction of himself and other managers he knows—than can be gained from secondhand interpretations. Third and by no means least in importance, veridical perception tends to produce greater involvement by management. Because the manager sees, hears, feels, ponders the facts himself and reacts emotionally, he develops a sense of commitment which is deeper than what he might get from hearsay. For purposes of creating support and enthusiasm for planning, this sense of commitment is tremendously important, for it means the executive will work harder to see the objectives are achieved and work hard more consistently through future periods of temporary discouragement and setback. One leader who knew the value of veridical perception was George H. Lesch, who became president of Colgate-Palmolive Company in 1960. For a number of years Colgate had been outsold by Procter & Gamble. Lesch reversed this; during the next five years Colgate's sales and earnings rose faster than P & G's. One of his unique talents seemed to be a good feel for trends in the market place. "The first thing he did on becoming president was to drop out of sight for three months, touring the U.S. to ask housewives and store managers for suggestions."[6]

Quantitative Analysis

While there may be no substitute for veridical perception, it does have its limitations. Weighing an observed reaction is difficult. How representative are the people you talk with? How typical are the facts you observe? Another limitation is bias. What you hear a person say may be what you wanted him to say before you ever talked with him. If so, you might as well have stayed in your office alone.

For reasons like these most executives who appraise skillfully try to combine veridical perception with statistical analyses

[6] *Forbes*, February 1, 1966, p. 29.

of organizational performance. The statistical analysis has weaknesses too; it is dry, one-dimensional, and lacking in the visceral detail that often gives one flashes of insight. But it is objective. The figures, if they are gathered with professional impartiality, do not contort conveniently in order to appease this particular bias or that. What is more, if the samples are carefully and repetitively drawn, they provide weights, depths, and perspectives which cannot otherwise be obtained. They tell you how serious this kind of complaint is, how widespread that form of satisfaction is, and what changes are occurring in both from period to period.

Alberto-Culver Company, the well-known manufacturer of hair preparations, first-aid items, dentifrices, and other products, has used figure analyses to size up its unique ability in promotion for purposes of investment and marketing planning. These analyses showed it was so accomplished in advertising that the more it invested in media, the more handsomely its advertising dollar paid off. By correlating sales and advertising expenditures, management learned that, once a brand was off the ground, its profitability grew faster than outlays on advertising increased.[7] Here indeed was an assessment of strength which carried more weight than eyewitness accounts ever could have done and which had immediate significance for program appropriations.

Usually, when analyses of this kind are made, it is the incremental contribution that management is interested in. That is, management is not so much concerned with broad averages of all sales, all profits on a product, all expenses including overhead for a certain project, or all investment including book value in a certain plant or facility; rather it tries to visualize the return resulting from an additional dollar spent today in a certain way.

While quantitative analysis has been pioneered in commercial business, it is being adopted more and more in nonprofit enterprises. A leader in voluntary health and welfare organizations

---

[7] Lee Adler, "A New Orientation for Plotting Marketing Strategy," *Business Horizons*, Winter, 1964, p. 41.

told of significant efforts that had been made in this field to quantify the value of services rendered. Admittedly, there was no way of quantifying reductions in human suffering or enhanced family happiness. Nevertheless, useful ways had been devised of analyzing the numbers of calls by social welfare workers, numbers of repeat visits necessary, number of children helped, and so forth, by types of organization and service. And from these quantifications some surprising insights had come for strategy concerning the strengths and weaknesses of voluntary private organizations in the field.

Personal Value Analysis

The term "value analysis" was first applied to purchasing, production, and marketing. It describes efforts to coordinate the three so that the end product meets the customer's specifications for performance and design at the lowest possible price. The aim of value analysis is to keep purchasing agents, production men, and marketers from setting standards for their work that are inconsistent with the needs of one another's functions.

The term "value analysis" is equally descriptive of an important job in strategic planning, that is, sizing up the values of key organizational people so that the goals and activities pursued reinforce these people's values and vice versa. It is probably fair to state that more waste can result from inconsistent managerial values and goals than from inconsistent purchasing, production, and marketing standards regarding materials and components of products.

Why do we discuss personal values in connection with organizational strengths and resources? Because, as indicated earlier, values are a decisive strength if they support the strategies selected. We need make no judgments at all as to whether a given set of values is good or bad. The organization could be an underworld army of dope peddlers, and it would not affect the question we are discussing here; if the values of that organization's leaders (however antisocial) are consistent with the planning objectives chosen, those values will be a vital resource in planning.

The question arises, therefore: How can management appraise values which affect the actions of executives and supervisors up and down the line? Several guides have been suggested by William D. Guth and Renato Tagiuri.[8] Their research shows, for example, that a manager can accomplish something simply by comparing his behavior, or an associate's, with the behavior of other men and women facing similar situations and problems. How much emphasis does he attach to purely "economic" results as opposed, let us say, to results which are desirable from a community viewpoint or from an employee human relations viewpoint? How much interest does he have in taking high risks at the cost of security and stability and vice versa?

Guth and Tagiuri emphasize that in making such appraisals the manager should be careful to take differences in information into account. Two men might be supporting divergent courses of action simply because of different understandings of the facts and problems involved. This may be why one chief executive I know of insists that the first rounds of questions at board meetings deal only with the *facts* of a proposal; evaluations and arguments over the desirability of the idea are not allowed until later.

Guth and Tagiuri believe that managers can also learn something about their values by taking certain kinds of tests. Such tests are designed to show the relative strength of different values held by an individual; the test scores should, of course, be analyzed by a professionally trained person.

But most important of all, in the opinion of the authors, is the manager's frame of mind in trying to size up his own and others'

[8] "Personal Values and Corporate Strategies," *Harvard Business Review*, September–October, 1965, p. 123.

values. The authors state that two requirements stand out in importance:

(1) There must be personal acceptance of the fact that his personal values are related to his implicit or explicit strategy choices. This will in itself make him more sensitive to what they are and how they may operate. Yet this may be a hard first step to take. Some of us have a difficult time accepting our personal involvement in situations, often insisting that we are being completely objective and that anyone who does not agree with us as to the validity and desirability of a particular strategic choice is simply "letting his emotions run away with him." Personal values are always involved in arriving at concepts of and "feels for" corporate strategies, and objectivity consists exactly of taking them into account, as we do with other elements in our analysis.

(2) There must be a willingness to focus on personal values as a possible explanation of differences among the concepts of corporate strategy held by various executives. Many of the same forces leading to the struggle for "objectiveness" in business practice lead to suppression of discussion of value differences among executives. The purpose of such discussion should not be to attempt to change anyone's values, a difficult task anyway, but rather to clarify the nature and source of differences and disagreements. It is often possible, through identification of similarities and differences in personal values, to cast up new strategy alternatives that will be more satisfying to all concerned than are those choices initially contributing to the conflict.[9]

Analyzing Markets

Now let us turn from internal analysis to external analysis—to the "out" part of inside-out planning. Unlike the tools of organizational self-appraisal, methods of evaluating markets, public needs, and economic conditions have received much attention in the literature, in educational programs, and at management meetings. The art of environmental analysis is also more sophisti-

[9] *Ibid.*, p. 130.

cated and advanced; some truly remarkable work has been done in this area, thanks to technological advances like the computer as well as to experiments in methodology.

General Variations

Some organizations rely primarily on personal judgments in market analysis. (In the case of nonprofit and governmental organizations, the more appropriate term "public need analysis" may be substituted for "market analysis.") For instance, Johns-Manville reportedly looks to its salesmen in the field to provide information on new markets, industries, and product developments, and it is from the salesmen that suggestions come for expanding into new markets or trying new products. The information is then evaluated by marketing managers, again on the basis of intuition and experience, and translated into planning. When the managers find themselves needing statistics or economic background, they can get it on request from a small planning staff.[10]

To refine personal judgments, but not so much as to take the intuition out of them, numerous organizations have developed special methods and directions. One company asks its division managers to make two sets of sales projections, one based on what they *feel sure* their divisions can do and the other based on what they *hope* to achieve. It is felt that such a distinction helps discipline the thinking of people developing estimates, making them more conscious of what is guesswork and what is not.

On the other hand, many successful organizations count heavily on statistical analysis in forecasting. For instance, Minnesota Mining and Manufacturing divides the world into 72 markets and its 10,000 products into 14 groups, for forecasting purposes. Every year the planners develop an estimate of product

---

[10] *Corporate Planning Today*, A Business International Research Report (New York: Business International Corporation, July, 1964), p. 53.

potential for each of the 14 groups in each of the 72 countries, with a point-value rating for each market. They base these estimates on correlations of economic and market factors which seem, from past experience, to be related to sales in the United States. Of course, final judgments by top management are made on the basis of experience and intuition, but obviously the quantitative analysis weighs heavily in the decision. As might be expected, the company has been making increasing use of computers for data processing.[11]

Special Techniques

One of the most interesting forecasting techniques is sensitivity analysis. This attempts to pick out the most important factors affecting demand and assess their impact. Just as in inside-out planning management tries to identify the talents and abilities most important to the future of the firm, so it now seeks to identify the most influential parts of the demand picture. There is this difference, of course: in the inside-out approach, management has power over the key factors (it can deliberately build them up, let them go undeveloped, or perhaps even destroy them), whereas in sensitivity analysis it acts more as a spectator. Always, though, the attempt to assess degrees of importance is a worth-while one, and particularly so in planning. It might be found, for instance, that the most critical factor in demand is one which the organization is especially well equipped to deal with, or just the opposite—either of which findings would bear on the amount of effort management decides to put into developing organizational abilities. If, let us say, the demand for a certain kind of steel is likely to be highly sensitive to price, it becomes important to ask if cost reduction, productive efficiency, and good labor–management relations are among the organization's special talents. If one or more of them are, an aggressive posture in this particular market makes more sense; if not, man-

[11] *Ibid.*

agement may wish to look harder at growth goals in some other area.

To make a sensitivity analysis, the forecasters take the most significant influences (such as, advertising, population growth, technological improvement, and the like) and decide what is most likely to happen to each influence. Suppose the plant produces office furniture. The forecasters would ask what the most likely future level and effectiveness of advertising will be in the office furniture industry, what the most likely number of potential buyers will be, what advances in design and materials are most likely, and so forth. Then they assume that these "most likely" levels will hold and, on that basis, predict demand for their line of office furniture. But suppose the "most likely" developments of the key factors do not in fact take place. It is therefore necessary to make projections of demand based on other assumptions; for instance, that advertising effort is restricted by high media prices, or that the number of new office buildings is not so great as generally expected, or that advances in design and materials greatly exceed present expectations. The forecasters predict what demand for their furniture will be in each event. The result is a set of projections showing how sensitive future demand is to different kinds of changes in the industry and market. The more sensitive it is, the more flexible the market programs should be.

A second technique of special interest here is what Lockheed Aircraft Corporation calls "prudent-manager forecasting." It is especially pertinent to industrial market forecasting. To use this technique, says Gerald A. Busch of Lockheed, management brings together a small group of seasoned specialists in such functions as marketing, finance, research, and production and asks them to assume the role of decision-making managers in a customer firm or group that is evaluating a product or service for purchase. The specialist's task is to review the facts available and arrive at preferred purchasing decisions from the *customer's* point of view. In effect, prudent-manager forecasting calls for a kind of role playing.

The "prudent managers" are given certain information representing the situation expected in the customer firm or firms: data on economic conditions, technology, logistics, and so forth. They are given information on the expected characteristics of the company's products and leading competitors' products (for example, in an aircraft manufacturer's case, data on the comparative speed, cost, and payload of different planes expected to be available on a certain date). And they are briefed in other ways, all to the end of enabling them to put themselves in the position of specific customers. Then they ask themselves what procurement policies they would follow at the future time in question, how the forecasting company's product stacks up against others on the market, how many of the product they would buy, what profits and return on investment they would expect to make, what operating problems they would be worrying about, and similar questions. They work out a forecast of what they would probably buy from the forecasting company, trying to do this as hardheadedly as if they were actually employees of the prospective buyer.

Having completed this prediction for one major customer, the "prudent managers" turn to another prospect and begin the same process all over again. When they have covered the whole field of major potential buyers, the expected purchases are totaled and this result is compared with any other forecasts made by the company staff. Lockheed managers believe they can get a better approximation this way of what may actually happen than they could with conventional staff forecasts.[12]

A Job for Generalists

Standing back from the immediate problems of strategic planning and looking at it in perspective, we notice a highly distinctive feature of it: *the changing points of view which are*

[12] See "Prudent Manager Forecasting," *Harvard Business Review*, May–June, 1961, p. 61.

necessary. There are times when it is essential for managers to take the viewpoint of the market, industry, community, or other part of the environment; there are other times when it is essential to develop the internal viewpoint of the people and facilities of the organization itself. Different management groups may prefer varying emphases, priorities, and orders of treatment of these two viewpoints, but always they will take both into account. Doing that is perhaps the most important requirement of all sound strategic planning.

People may debate the relative merits of the inside-out and outside-in approaches. They may disagree over the relative potentials of statistical as opposed to qualitative forecasting. They may have contrasting notions of the importance of taking personal values into account. They may argue about how best to develop organizational abilities and relate them to the needs of users and buyers. They may differ over questions of method: sensitivity analysis, prudent-manager prediction, numerically weighted judgments for computer processing, use of salesmen's judgments, and hundreds of others.

Such differences of opinion are to be expected and, managed with reasonable judgment, may contribute to organizational creativity. But about the need for taking a dual point of view in setting goals there is no valid argument. This has to be done if the goals are to be well thought out. The challenge is to be able to alternate between views and standpoints, to shift from one to another and back again, to be able to work both sides of the street.

Strategic planning can never, therefore, be delegated largely to specialists (however much they can contribute to the solution of particular problems). It is the responsibility of the generalists in management.

Leverage from Budgeting

7

Early in 1969 the "Jonesville" Division of an Illinois corporation estimates sales of $12 million in 1970 for its cable products and sales of $15 million in 1971. Rough pen-and-pencil computations by the controller show that $2.7 million profit should be gained in 1970, if there are no unexpected changes in the price and cost picture, and $3.2 million in 1971. On the basis of these "guesstimates," profitability before taxes looks satisfactory (22.5 and 21 per cent), so the controller is given the go-ahead to draw up a more precise budget using the same price-cost assumptions. (The division was an independent small company until recently and still operates very much like an autonomous organization.)

Working first with the sales manager, the controller asks for careful estimates of what each salesman expects to sell during the budget periods; these estimates are to be broken down by type of cable, price, sales area, and type of customer (construction, manufacturing, municipal, and so on). When these data come in, the controller and sales manager go over them item by item. Some figures do not look right, so the sales manager calls in the salesmen who submitted them and clears up the questions. A few estimates seem too optimistic, so the controller and sales manager adjust them downward. A fair number of estimates seem too conservative and are adjusted upward (the sales manager says, "Those men always like to look good by exceeding their targets").

Entering a second stage of discussions with the sales head, the controller writes down tentative price projections based on the best intelligence available concerning major competitors, metal price trends, and so forth. Some of the points in these price discussions remind him and the sales manager of weak figures in the volume projections, so they go back over a few of their earlier estimates and alter them.

Leaving the sales department, the controller goes to Jonesville's production executives. Once again, costs are computed item by item, sometimes simply on the basis of trends in the past few years, sometimes on that basis combined with predictions of the outcome of negotiations with the union and of current talks with suppliers. (Some of the production men have different notions about supplier price trends than the sales manager did, so the controller puts a question mark over a few price projections earlier made.) When these cost projections turn out to be higher than expected in the tentative budget made at the outset of budget discussions, the controller goes back to the sales manager, and together they try to stretch or contract various sales projections in such a way that the original profitability targets can still be met. This effort is only partially successful. Notes are made of the reasons why.

When the controller has all his facts and estimates assembled in a thorough budget document, he goes to the division vice-president for final approval. In the vice-president's office, he knows, the whole document will be gone over again critically, with the possibility that still more rounds of talks with sales and manufacturing executives may become necessary.

Clearly, some of the things that the executives of the Jonesville Division are doing in this budgeting effort are the same kinds of thing they do in planning as described in earlier chapters. Budgeting is a potent tool of planning. While it is often possible to make good plans without budgeting, it is not often possible to have good *planning* without budgeting, especially in the operational and implementational phases, for budgeting reinforces many activities that make planning a real and vital process. It produces the personal interplay, negotiation, practicality, and specificity which are so essential to the decision-making dimension of planning (this dimension is what makes planning different from plans, which do not necessarily embody decision making). More than that, budgeting makes contributions to planning that can be made by no other process.

Ralph F. Lewis of Arthur Young and Company describes the work as follows:

Budgeting is the process of expressing in units and dollars the plans for a business for a specific period of time, usually a year. It is the means by which conflicting goals of various departments may be modified so that the best interest of the enterprise as a whole may be achieved. In a small, one-man operation, it may be possible to "get by" without reducing overall plans to quantitative terms. On the other hand, even smaller businesses are becoming extremely complex, to the point that some systematic process of getting figures down on paper is increasingly essential if all areas of a business are to be harnessed toward overall company aims.[1]

Of course, in this field as in so many others we have problems of nomenclature. Budgeting is not always called that. Executives may feel an antipathy toward the term and use some other one instead: "operating plan," perhaps, or "P & L forecast." Here we shall simply use the traditional name, budgeting, and let readers substitute another term if they want to. It also should be mentioned that there are many kinds of budgets. There are cash budgets, variable budgets, program budgets, organization budgets, and others. A few of these distinctions are important here;

[1] *Management Uses of Accounting: Planning and Control for Profit* (New York: Harper, 1961), p. 2.

most are not. We shall consider only some general aspects of the subject as it relates to making planning work, leaving other aspects for books that describe budgeting in more detail.[2] How does budgeting help planning? How can it become more useful? What conflicts are there between budgeting and planning?

Aid to Communication

A perennial pitfall in planning is inadequate communication. Budgeting helps management avoid this pitfall because it makes executives pin their estimates down. Overhead will not simply be "up" next year; it will be greater by $23,500, or 3.4 per cent. Equipment purchases will not be "about the same" next year; they will be $114,900, or 0.4 per cent less than this year. And so forth.

Because executives' estimates of feelings about the future must be pinned down in number form and sometimes also in the form of precise facts appended to the numerical summaries, there is more chance that a true meeting of the minds will be obtained as to what the company expects to happen. Some managers would go further than this. They would say that budgeting leads to the creation of formal communication *channels* for designing, revising, and transmitting plans. In their budgeting work, members of an organization make certain "paths" back and forth between themselves: habits of asking and answering questions, mutual understandings concerning what must be done, and so forth. These "paths" serve the whole planning process.

How can the potential value of budgeting as a communication tool be increased? In general, the answer would seem to be more employee participation in budgeting, more involvement. To be

2 See, for example, Burnard H. Sord and Glenn A. Welsch, *Business Budgeting* (New York: Controllership Foundation, Inc., 1958 and 1962); David Novick, editor, *Program Budgeting: Program Analysis and the Federal Budget* (Cambridge: Harvard University Press, 1966); Herman C. Heiser, *Budgeting Principles and Practice* (New York: Ronald Press, 1959); and Ralph F. Lewis, *op. cit.*

sure, companies seem to do quite well in getting all *levels* of management to participate in the process. In a leading study, 83 per cent of 35 companies where personal interviews were conducted, and 85 per cent of 389 companies queried by questionnaire, reported that budgets were first submitted by subordinate levels to higher levels; moreover, practically none of the companies reported that higher-level executives established goals and objectives for budgets without consulting their subordinates first.[3] But various *functions* are often poorly represented in budget formulation. In the study just mentioned, for instance, less than half of the companies reported establishing definite budget objectives regarding numbers of employees and credit collections, and barely more than half set such objectives for purchasing.[4]

The communication value of budgeting could also be improved if some of the newer forms of this tool were used more widely. The vast majority of industrial companies now use profit-and-loss budgets, most of them divided into monthly time periods. However, there appears to be much less use of program budgeting, which is particularly pertinent to planning because it means that costs and incomes for a future period are "packaged" according to the end results desired—marketing goals for specific products and processes, investment goals for real estate acquisitions, share-of-market goals in a new industry being entered, or whatever other objectives are sought. It is significant that the federal government is buying the program approach. Stimulated by the pioneering efforts of the Department of Defense, the Rand Corporation, and others (actually, DuPont appears to have first used the principle, in the very early 1920's), a number of agencies are working on so-called planning-programming-budgeting systems in which a planned activity or "mission" is stated (if possible, in quantitative terms), alternative means for accomplishing it are spelled out, and cost estimates are at-

[3] Sord and Welsch, *op. cit.*, p. 97.
[4] *Ibid.*, p. 88.

tached to the alternatives. The more that approaches like this are used, the more budgeting can contribute to clear, precise, thorough understanding of an organization's planning.

Tool for Evaluation

There is another way in which budgeting—program budgeting in particular—can add leverage to management's efforts to make planning work. As described by Robert N. Anthony:

> This type of budget [a program budget] is useful to an executive examining the overall balance among the various programs of the business. It helps to answer such questions as these: Is the profit margin on each product line satisfactory? Is production capacity in balance with the size and capability of the sales organization? Can we afford to spend so much for research? Are adequate funds available? And so on. A negative answer to any of these questions indicates the necessity for revising the plan.[5]

Frederick C. Mosher saw related advantages when he made these observations a number of years ago:

> Planning involves first the conceiving of goals and the development of alternative courses of future action to achieve the goals. Second, it involves the reduction of these alternatives from a very large number to a small number and finally to one approved course of action, *the program*. Budgeting probably plays a slight part in the first phase but an increasingly important and decisive part in the second. It facilitates the choice-making process by providing a basis for systematic comparisons among alternatives which take into account their total impacts on both the debit and the credit sides. It thus encourages, and provides some of the tools for, an increasing degree of precision in the planning process. Budgeting is the ingredient of planning which disciplines the entire process.[6]

---

[5] *Management Accounting Principles* (Homewood, Ill.: Richard D. Irwin, 1965), p. 266.

[6] *Program Budgeting* (Chicago: Public Administration Service, 1954), pp. 48–49.

How can management maximize the value of budgeting for evaluating plans and programs? One way is to define clearly and explicitly the cardinal assumptions and expectations on which a budget, and hence at least part of a program, are based. For instance, what supporting services—legal, research, personnel, editorial, and so forth—does the organization plan to give the sales, manufacturing, and purchasing departments? What components or materials of an end product does the company intend to buy, and in what quantities, and what does it intend to make? What channels of distribution will be used?

Better Coordination of Effort

Budgeting would help managers, departments, and groups coordinate their efforts if it did no more than improve communication, as previously described. Perhaps its most important contribution to coordination, however, is a more substantive one. While it focuses the attention of managers and groups on their own immediate objectives, it also should lead them to consider how those objectives fit into the over-all departmental or corporate picture. For instance, a production manager can look at a sales budget, if it is properly detailed (and especially if it is done in program form), and tell what output is expected from him, and when, in order to meet the marketing plan. Similarly, a traffic manager can take a production budget and a marketing budget, if they are properly prepared, and learn much about the demands that will be placed on him for transportation and distribution during the budget periods.

In many organizations the potentials of budgeting for this purpose can probably be exploited more than they are at present. It is true that senior budgeting and planning officials of most companies coordinate the objectives and goals of different organizational units in over-all corporate budgets.[7] However, the managers of individual departments and projects too often see their budgets only as limitations, with little or no recognition

---

[7] Sord and Welsch, *op. cit.*, p. 103.

of how the documents are coordinated. The production man does not *see* that his budget dovetails with the sales manager's and warehouse manager's budgets in certain indicated ways, and vice versa. "Corporate results achieved under circumstances such as these can differ widely from those budgeted" notes J. H. Hennessy, Jr., "and yet each department head may feel satisfied that he has fulfilled his budget obligations."[8] Under circumstances like these, it does no good that people's involvement in budget making increases their sense of commitment to budgeted goals; that sense of commitment may only make matters worse.

What is needed, therefore, is more effort on the part of budgeting and planning people to show operating people how their budgets relate to one another—how these relationships can be read from the budget documents. Naturally, this effort will be easier, as already indicated, if budgets are drawn in the newer program form rather than in the older forms (expense budgets, with expenses collected in categories like salaries, raw materials, transportation, and so on, and functional budgets, with costs and incomes categorized by organizational functions like sales, purchasing, advertising, manufacturing). Also needed are efforts to make sure budgets are reviewed frequently enough and revised at appropriate intervals. In the Financial Executives Research Foundation survey, over half of the several hundred companies reported reviewing budgets for possible revision on a quarterly or monthly basis. In the great majority of companies, the fact that budgets are divided into monthly intervals makes it possible to have a review on fairly short notice if performance figures can be reported rapidly and are consistent with the budget categories.

Aid to Control

In the minds of many executives, budgeting has unmatched value as a tool of control. It helps them keep on top of efforts to

---

[8] "Looking Around: Budgets for Management," *Harvard Business Review,* May–June, 1960, p. 36.

achieve planned objectives and to keep abreast of special problems and opportunities. For instance, Textron asks each division
to prepare a twelve-month budget; each budget is checked every
month against the division's operating results, and every quarter
revisions are considered. In addition, each year a division pre-
pares a fresh five-year forecast which shows what personnel
and facilities it expects to need, what new products it plans to be
producing, what markets it intends to work in, and so forth.
When its operations depart from the long-term forecast, that is a
flag to top management that something different from expectations is happening which calls for a talk with division managers.
At this company, in other words, budgeting is what makes
"management by exception" possible, which in turn assists in
implementing company programs.

Robert N. Anthony maintains that the responsibility budget
is the form that is most appropriate for control:

> The responsibility budget sets forth plans in terms of the persons
> responsible for carrying them out. It is therefore primarily a control
> device, since it is a statement of expected or standard perform-
> ance against which actual performance can later be compared. In the
> factory, for example, there may be a responsibility budget for each
> department, showing the costs that are controllable by the foreman of
> the department. There may also be a budget showing costs for each
> product, including both direct costs and allocated costs. The figures
> on both sets of budgets add up to total factory costs, but the product-
> cost budget would not be useful for control purposes, since the costs
> shown on it could not ordinarily be related to the responsibility of
> specific individuals.[9]

When controllable costs are shown separately, the effect of
a department's management on operations is not confused with
factors beyond its control (for example, material costs or transfer prices in the case of a manufacturing department). Also,
it is wise to establish budget standards that management considers reasonably attainable, so that any difference between the

[9] Robert N. Anthony, *op. cit.*, p. 266.

standard and actual performance represents a true variance—a slip or gain in the plan. (If management uses budgets also as incentives, setting the standards higher than ordinary in order to stimulate extraordinary performance toward an ideal, it should distinguish the incentive standards from control standards.)

Dangers

In both industry and government (and probably in other fields, too) budgeters and planners knock heads together noisily every so often, each accusing the other of congenital inability. As far as budgeting is concerned, however, one gets the feeling that real and steady improvements are being made from a planner's point of view.

The rise of program budgeting in addition to or in place of functional budgets; the steady growth of profit-and-loss budgets; increasing recognition of such needs as separating controllable from noncontrollable costs and keeping cost categories in responsibility budgets consistent with cost categories in the accounts where performance is reported—these and other trends are giving budgeting a more useful cast from a planning standpoint. And various trends in planning—particularly those bringing planning into the context of daily decision making, as described in previous chapters—should help that function become more acceptable from a budgeter's standpoint.

Nevertheless, several dangers stand in the way of rapprochement. One of these is the tendency to *equate* budgeting and planning. According to E. Kirby Warren, this tendency is most pronounced among managers with finance and accounting backgrounds.[10] While budgeting and planning are interconnected, they are separate in principle as well as in detail. Failure to appreciate this can lead only to trouble. As such authorities as George A. Steiner have repeatedly emphasized, budgets are highly useful management tools, but only one part of the whole

[10] *Long-Range Planning* (Englewood Cliffs, N.J.: Prentice-Hall, 1966), p. 17.

planning process. Goals and strategies cannot properly be framed on the basis of current budgetary decisions. Budgets may manifest management intentions and help in their crystallization, but they lack the total involvement which general plans and programs have.

A second danger is the temptation to call on budgeting officers to handle planning assignments. Some budget officers are well equipped to make the transition to planning, but good work in budgeting is no assurance of readiness for planning responsibilities. If planning decisions are viewed as a spectrum, like radio frequencies, there is in this spectrum a very broad "band" which is highly qualitative. There is no necessary relationship between proficiency in this qualitative band and proficiency in quantitative analysis or accounting.

Why are such obvious differences in requirements overlooked? Perhaps the explanation is that budgeting is well institutionalized, and its practices well established, whereas planning is not. Unlike budgeting, the practice of planning varies drastically from company to company, depending on local needs and personalities; planning practices also change from time to time within a given company as needs, personalities, and the state of the art change (budgeting does not change so much in this way either). The variability of planning will probably lessen in the future as the art assumes more definite form, and then it will take on clearer meaning in people's minds. But for the present, at least, budgeting managers are associated with a more tangible, more recognizable discipline than are people called "corporate planners."

A third set of dangers has to do with the concept of budgeting itself. Foremost among these is the notion that a budget is a kind of forecast. If it were, it would still be useful to planning; forecasts generally are. But it would have nowhere near the value that it does when more properly conceived as a statement of intended management *action*, that often calls for *changing* the future from the present. A budget may properly call for a reduction in overhead expense despite the fact that overhead costs in the industry or locality are expected to rise; it may properly call for an increase in sales revenue even though forecasts show that the market as a whole will contract and most companies' volumes will fall. A budget may do such things if it reflects definite management desires to move in these directions coupled with a specific set of actions to implement the desire. So conceived, it obviously has much greater utility as a tool of planning than any forecast can.

The Marvelous Power of
Quantitative Tools

8

Literally speaking, the title of this chapter is a misnomer. It is not really the methods of quantitative analysis themselves that have such great power, but the mind of the person using them. What the tools do is help extend the reaches and perceptiveness of the managerial mind, just as machine tools enable a worker to accomplish more with his hands. So when we speak of what quantitative analysis can do, we are simply using literary license to advertise an opportunity.

Enormous strides have been made in developing quantitative methods for management use. Someday ages from now when its history can be seen in long perspective, it will probably be written that of all the applications of mathematics—to physics, chemistry, architecture, space travel, and the rest—few had more profound influence on professional practice than the relatively simple, eminently practical methods developed for management. They are useful, as we shall see, for strategic analysis as well as for evaluating methods of implementing plans. They are valuable for the numerical answers they give as well as for their use simply in stretching a manager's thinking. They show him roads to explore that he might not otherwise have looked at. They lead him to make judgments that he might otherwise have shrugged off. They add enormously to his flexibility and versatility, enabling him to test combinations of alternatives and possibilities which would otherwise be too unwieldy to test. What is more, many businessmen have reported that quantitative methods help them in communicating with associates just as much, in their opinion, as methods of better oral presentation or personal salesmanship. The reason is that a quantitative approach is likely to precipitate an open and probing discussion of a problem simply because the numerical requirements, like impartial arbiters, demand it.

Many of the quantitative tools developed in recent years have just as much application to the needs of a smaller company—even a one- or two-man company—as to the needs of a large business, university, or government organization.

In this chapter we shall review just a few methods. They are chosen to suggest the extent and kinds of assistance obtainable for planning, and the omission of others in no way indicates that the latter are less important. To set the stage, let us make note of several key assumptions and notions that underlie the use of quantitative methods in general.

Some Key Assumptions and Notions

First, in discussions of quantitative methods, a commonly made assumption is that the user seeks to *maximize the profits* of the division or corporation. This may be a perfectly realistic assumption, and as such it is wonderfully convenient. For different dollar results are the easiest kind of results to compare; also, dollars are ready-made units of value to use in computations which cannot, of course, begin to be made at all until inputs are expressed numerically.

However, it is not essential that profit maximization be the goal. This is fortunate, for it means that nonbusiness organizations can use quantitative methods, too, as many of them long have done. What is more, there is a growing impression among observers of the corporate scene that profit objectives often take their place alongside—not always above—other kinds of objective.

Objectives other than profit are often expressed in numerical terms. The Department of Defense expresses many of its goals in terms of firepower; telephone companies have service goals that take the form of numbers of users, costs to users, and waiting time; the objective in a logistics problem may be to find some combination of routes, warehousing capacity, and shipping requirements that makes economical distribution possible; and so on. The effect of various actions and events on these objectives can usually be estimated or measured, with the result that quantitative methods may be helpful.

Even if objectives are not ordinarily expressed in numerical terms, it may be possible to do so for purposes of mathematical analysis. The management of a company might, for instance, have such goals as being technological leader in the industry and enjoying high respect in the community, in addition to its profit goals. It might be able to express the first two in terms of the last —deciding, say, that investments rated as "highly valuable," "moderately valuable," and "slightly valuable" for purposes of technological leadership are worth $250,000, $150,000, and $50,000, respectively, in terms of increased corporate profits; while investments similarly rated for their community relations value are worth $150,000, $100,000, and $25,000, respectively (see Exhibit II). A set of investment alternatives can then be compared in terms of their contribution to each of these goals and a numerically "best" investment thereby determined. Thus, investment A, which is considered "moderately valuable" for industry technological leadership and community relations goals and is estimated as likely to add $300,000 to profits, would rank under investment B, which should add $400,000 to profits but

Exhibit II. Equivalent Worth of Investments

Estimated Value for Technological Leadership or Community Relations*	Equivalent Worth in Profits[†]	
	Technological Leadership	Community Relations
High	$250,000	$150,000
Moderate	150,000	100,000
Slight	50,000	25,000

*Estimated by experts in areas
†Estimated by top management

be only "slightly valuable" for technological leadership and community relations.

In actual practice, scales with more gradations would be used so that values between "highly," "moderately," and "slightly" could be selected by managers doing the rating. Also, as Exhibit II suggests, it may be wise to procure different estimates from different groups (for instance, equivalent worth figures from senior operating executives and specific functional ratings of different possible investments from experts in the areas in question).

A *second* assumption commonly made in discussions of quantitative methods is that *alternative goals and/or means exist for the user.* This is an increasingly realistic assumption in advanced industrial economies. Typically, a food chain considers a number of good locations for a new store, a mutual fund can grow at different speeds depending on how aggressively it promotes itself and advertises, and a manufacturer has a variety of possible product lines and investment opportunities to select from in its three- to five-year planning.

A *third* assumption necessary in many forms of quantitative analysis is that *probabilities of success* (or of other results) can be attached by management to future actions and events. Here we may run into trouble. As those who have worked in this field know all too well, managers are often reluctant to make probability estimates. They balk at stating that in their opinion, let us say, new product A has a 60 per cent chance of earning $100,000 or more, a 30 per cent chance of earning $150,000 or more, and a 10 per cent chance of earning $200,000 or more. Nevertheless, there is steadily growing recognition in the management community that probability estimates must and can be made for planning. As one executive of a manufacturing concern said (his management was swinging around to this viewpoint only after holding out against it for many years), "Unless we define the risks of a proposed investment, what sense does it make to compare a proposal having a high probability of a 12 per cent return with a proposal having a low probability of a 16 per cent return?"

If staff specialists or outside consultants carry out the quantitative analysis, it is vital that the probabilities they use be acceptable to top management. At the Harvard Business School, Professor Pearson Hunt uses a case in which a planning department of a company made an elaborate investment analysis. All the important variables were labeled, probabilities were assigned to different levels of expected return, cash flows were worked out by computer, and so forth. After spending many weeks on this analysis, the planners gave the company president their recommendation. He rejected it within an hour. The reason? He could not accept the probability estimates which the planners had cranked into their study. Those estimates had not been worked out first with him.

A *fourth* assumption often made is that *money has a time value:* for instance, that $100,000 of income expected one year from now is equivalent to a little less than that in terms of current income, while $100,000 of income expected two years from now is worth less still, and so on into the future. The logic behind this notion of present value or discounted earnings is, of course, that if an organization were to take $95,238 today and invest it at 5 per cent, let us say, its money would grow to $100,000 in one year (compounded annually), while only $90,703 invested today would grow to $100,000 in two years (and so on). The appropriate discount rate to use varies. Sometimes the organization's over-all cost of capital is used; sometimes other figures are employed.

It is not always essential to discount future earnings. The adjustment is easy to make, however (discount tables can be obtained from various sources, including some texts), and discounting does have a near-irrefutable logic when cost or income figures at different points in time are being compared.

Aside from its logic, the present value concept has other advantages for planning. It tends to make managers more "future-oriented." It tends to center their attention on years to come rather than on the past, on the anticipated net gains of possible new investments rather than on writing off costs of investments made in years gone by.

With these assumptions in mind, let us turn to specific methods of analysis.

Decision Trees

The term "decision tree" was invented to reflect the fact that today's decision depends partly on the decisions and choices we expect to have tomorrow. Between now and then we shall be learning facts that will influence the choices we actually make tomorrow. As we look into the future, we see an ever-enlarging growth of possibilities and choices, a proliferating tree of branches beyond and above the alternatives faced today.

The purpose of a decision-tree analysis is to help the executive make today's decisions with a perceptive view of their impact on the choices he will have tomorrow. In its essence, therefore, the tree concept embodies the spirit of planning as earlier defined in this book. When diagramed on paper, a decision tree includes both events or results of action and management choices as to what action to take. It does not reveal what is the best decision to make, but only which alternative will provide the greatest gain in view of the probabilities foreseen. It is a superb tool for forcing into the open managerial assumptions about the future, for stimulating discussion of differing opinions and values, for encouraging "second looks" at plans with an eye to needed revision. It clarifies information needs for planning decisions. It highlights risks.

As might be expected, in view of these advantages, the decision-tree method is likely to lead managers to make different decisions—and better ones—than they would make without it. Its use is no guarantee of successful decision making, naturally, for probability estimates can be wrong, and unlikely or unanticipated events can always upset the picture; besides, making the best bets is no promise of winning, anyway, since the probabilities can go against you.

Characteristics

Business executives have used decision trees to help them decide what type of factory to build for a new manufacturing project, how to modernize a plant, whether to develop a new product, and similar questions. In what many businessmen consider the outstanding exposition of decision trees, John F. Magee of Arthur D. Little, Inc., shows how a decision tree can even help you decide whether to plan a large cocktail party indoors or outdoors;[1] and once when I was discussing decision trees with some students, they showed me a tree diagram (sketched on a table mat) for deciding whether to go out next Saturday with a blind date from Radcliffe or a blind date from Wellesley.

Essentially, as Magee shows, a decision tree involves four steps:

[1] "Decision Trees for Decision Making," *Harvard Business Review*, July–August, 1964, p. 126. This first article was followed by a second, "How to Use Decision Trees in Capital Investment," *Harvard Business Review*, September–October, 1964, p. 79. Both articles are drawn on for purposes of this discussion.

1. Identifying the problem and the alternatives at various stages of action.

2. Laying out the decision tree in diagram form.

3. Obtaining the needed facts and figures regarding probabilities, costs, cash flows, sales, profits, losses, and so on.

4. Evaluating the alternatives (which may well lead to revising or redrawing the tree).

How much detail is used? How elaborately are these steps done? That depends on the situation. Some decision questions boil down to a simple, one-time choice between alternatives, whereas others are complex and multistage. Generally speaking, though, a second stage of decision-tree making—that is, drawing out the tree to the decision choices and consequences which will result at a future time directly from the choices made today— is desirable because it enriches the present with the future. On the other hand, there comes a point, sometime around the fourth or fifth "generation" of choices and results, when the tree will burgeon too far with possibilities and probabilities.

A related rule is that the time period covered depends on how far into the future there are visible decision choices that significantly influence today's choices. For a merchandising problem, the time span might appropriately be only eighteen months; but for a research and development problem it might be ten years. (It is for similar reasons that many of us find it hard to define "short-," "intermediate-," and "long-"range planning in terms of years.)

A third general rule is that you do not try to outline every possible choice, result, and contingency. You deal with the more important ones only.

Note that each of these general rules is a good discipline for the planner. Each tends to keep his eye on the primary decisions and consequences and on a practical, manageable time period. If this is not done—if, instead, plans turn either into detailed engineering-type blueprints or into "blue-sky" jobs—planning will probably lose its flexibility, vitality, and capacity to stimulate action.

One does not work with decision trees very long before tripping once or twice over the question of probabilities. At a minimum, the need for a probability estimate will precipitate differences of opinion as to what will happen; at worst, the need will lead to arguments over the very role of probability estimates. Nevertheless, probability has a crucial role in the decision-tree approach. Magee states:

Those engaged in the analysis should be encouraged to express doubts and uncertainties and to express estimates of costs, technical feasibility, or forecasts of market conditions in terms of *ranges* or *probabilities*. Much as management might wish the uncertainties would go away, undue criticism of the analyst for being imprecise or insufficiently firm in his estimates will only force the uncertainties and the risks underground. The purpose of the investment analysis is to help management identify alternatives and bring out the facts about them.[2]

As might be expected, probabilities must often be estimated by seasoned executives on the basis of experience. Illustrations of such probabilities are the likelihood that a competitor will succeed or fail on a certain research project which will change the market picture for the company's product, or that the company will be able to cooperate successfully with another firm on a joint venture being considered. But other probabilities can be estimated objectively by experts, be they experienced managers or not. For instance, the chances that damages in an antitrust suit will be nearer $10,000 than $50,000 can be figured by lawyers, and the chances that buyers in the El Paso region will prefer a new color TV set to black-and-white sets by a two-to-one margin can be estimated by market researchers in the southwest. The manager never has to feel stuck with one probability estimate, however. He can experiment with several, using each in a set of computations and seeing how it affects the outcome.

[2] Magee, "How to Use Decision Trees in Capital Investment," *op. cit.*, p. 80.

Managers in government and business often balk at "making a production" of gathering probability estimates, especially when some guesswork is involved. Magee's answer is a persuasive one:

What is gained by trying to make subjective estimates of probabilities where limited objective information exists? Why not make the decision on feel, hunch, or intuition in the first place? For one thing, the estimation of elemental probabilities (and other values) permits various parties to the decision to see the basis for each other's conclusions. For another, it permits the executive to make use of the intuitions and skills of subordinate operators as staff members without abdicating his position as the decision-maker. Further, it permits analysis of the impact of variations in the estimate—what is called *sensitivity analysis*.[3]

Most users of decision trees discount future cash flows by some appropriate rate and enter expected future values at their present values. Discounting is not, however, a requirement of decision trees and may, at management's discretion, be omitted from the analysis (as in the illustration which follows on page 121).

Procedures

Suppose we are managers in a company making a sunscreen, and we are discussing whether to try to develop a new line of screen that must be produced (if possible) on machines not yet devised but considered feasible. If the machines can be completed as we hope they can be, we may gain an advantage over competitors in the sunscreen and room-conditioning business, but we are not sure we can pull the development off successfully. The trouble is that if we do not do it, a competitor may, and if he does we are afraid he will cut into sales of our present lines of screen. How would we go about using the decision-tree method to help us clarify the opportunities and risks and make the best decision we can with today's knowledge?

[3] *Ibid.*, p. 86.

First, of course, we must delineate the problem. We can author-ize the development project or not authorize it. If we do authorize it, we may succeed or we may not succeed. If we succeed, we will have the option then of going into production or, if facts gained in the interim give us second thoughts about market potentials then, delay production or shelve the whole project. If we go into production, demand may turn out to be high or low. Whether it is high or low, a competitor may or may not join us in the market with a similar new kind of sunscreen. And so on.

After talking over these possibilities and trying to visualize the most important ones, we might lay out a tree diagram like that shown in Exhibit III. In the first version we would outline the limbs only, without any figures. And we would probably re-vise the tree several times before agreeing that it represents the situation as well as possible right now. To distinguish decisions from events (market demand, competitor's actions, outcome of our development work, and so on), we use a square for the former and a circle for the latter.

Next we would try to get some figures to put on the tree. What are the chances the project will succeed, if we undertake it? Some of us will be optimistic, others pessimistic, and it will not be easy to set a figure. For an analysis satisfactory to everyone, we may want to draw up several trees with different estimates of this probability. Let us suppose, though, that one such esti-mate is a 70 per cent chance of success. We would use that figure for the first pair of branches on the upper limb: .70 for one branch, .30 for the other. Then we would begin asking ourselves about the probabilities that market demand will be high or low (we could put in more alternatives, if we wanted—high, medium high, medium, medium low, low, and so on) and the probabilities whether a competitor will succeed with a new screen too. Let us say that one likely estimate is an 80 per cent chance of high demand and a 70 per cent chance that a competitor will come on the market with a new screen. Putting these estimates on the tree, we might draw two upper branches for high demand, one

Exhibit III. Decision Tree for New Screen Project

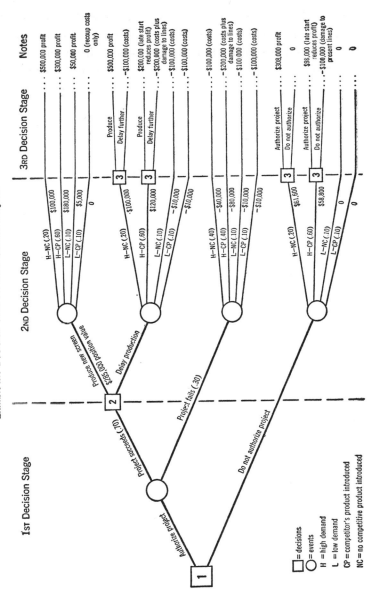

1ST Decision Stage	2ND Decision Stage	3RD Decision Stage	Notes

1ST Decision Stage

2ND Decision Stage

3RD Decision Stage

Notes

Authorize project

Do not authorize project

Project succeeds (.70)

Project fails (.30)

Produce new screen

$285,000 position value

Delay production

H–NC (.20) $100,000 ... $500,000 profit
H–CP (.60) $180,000 ... $300,000 profit
L–NC (.10) $5,000 ... $50,000 profit.
L–CP (.10) 0 ... 0 (recoup costs only)

H–NC (.20) –$100,000 ... Produce ... $500,000 profit
... Delay further ... –$100,000 (costs)
H–CP (.60) $120,000 ... Produce ... $200,000 (late start reduces profit)
... Delay further ... –$200,000 (costs plus damage to lines)
L–NC (.10) –$10,000 ... –$100,000 (costs)
L–CP (.10) –$10,000 ... –$100,000 (costs)

H–NC (.40) –$40,000 ... –$100,000 (costs)
H–CP (.40) –$80,000 ... –$200,000 (costs plus damage to lines)
L–NC (.10) –$10,000 ... –$100,000 (costs)
L–CP (.10) –$10,000 ... –$100,000 (costs)

H–NC (.20) $61,800 ... Authorize project ... $308,000 profit
... Do not authorize ... 0
H–CP (.60) $58,800 ... Authorize project ... $98,000 (late start reduces profit)
... Do not authorize ... –$100,000 (damage to present lines)
L–NC (.10) 0 ... 0
L–CP (.10) 0 ... 0

☐ = decisions
◯ = events
H = high demand
L = low demand
CP = competitor's product introduced
NC = no competitive product introduced

showing high demand and the chance a competitor will market a new screen (the .60 limb), one showing high demand without the competitor's screen (the .20 limb—the two representing the 80 per cent probability); two other branches show low demand without the competitor's presence (a .10 limb) and low demand with the competitor's rivalry in the market (another .10 limb). As these figures indicate, we consider the chances heavy that a competitor will come on the market only if demand is high.

Now look at the "delay production" branch in Exhibit III. To the far right, you will see two sets of small branches not shown on the upper part of the tree. We draw these to represent the possibility that, if we postpone production at first, we will want to change our minds if we find that demand is high and launch into production then. Similarly, down near the bottom, to the right of the "do not authorize" limb, you will see two sets of small branches representing a change of heart; if we decide against the project today, we may want to authorize it later on when new facts show us demand is high.

Note that the probabilities for events in the second decision stage are generally the same down through the tree, indicating our judgment that the market will be high or low regardless of what we decide to do and that a competitor is just as likely to go ahead with his development project if we also go ahead as if we do not. But there is one exception: if our project fails, we think he is more likely to fail, too. That is, if there are technical difficulties that block us, they may well deter him as well. Hence on the "project fails" limb we put only a 40 per cent chance of the competitor's marketing a new product if demand is high and a 10 per cent chance if demand is low.

In addition to probabilities we want figures on profits and costs. It is likely that the development work will cost $100,000. If it succeeds, if demand is high, and if there is no rival screen on the market, we should take in $600,000 profits in a three-year period (three years, let us say, is the longest period of profit taking we want to allow for, even though with luck profits will continue longer); subtracting development costs from that figure gives us $500,000, as shown in the top right corner of the tree. On the other hand, if demand is high and a competitor does come out with a screen like ours, we predict a net profit after development costs of $300,000.

If the development work succeeds but we postpone production for a while, and no competitive product comes on the market, we will still make $500,000 if we launch production later (see decision stage #3).

Suppose we decide against undertaking the development work today, but want to do so later when we learn that demand is really going to be very good. This possibility is shown at the lower right of the tree (ends of the "do not authorize" limb). If we decide then to authorize the development, we estimate the same cash flows as in the top sections *if* no competitor comes on the scene ($308,000 is the product of $500,000 multiplied by the .70 chance of development success, less the cost of project failure, $42,000, which is computed by multiplying the four possible losses of $140,000 by the .30 chance of failure). But if a competitor has come out with a new product in the meantime, so that we are second on the market instead of first or simultaneous (as at the top), then we do not think our profits will be so great. Let us say our best guess is that coming on the market second will mean $100,000 less profits. Then we would have $200,000 profits (instead of $300,000 as at the top), which, when multiplied by the 70 per cent chance of development success, and with $42,000 deducted, gives us $98,000. If demand for the new product is low, a competitor's launching of it will not hurt our present lines.

Suppose we do not put the new screen on the market at all, for one reason or another, but a competitor does. Then we estimate a drain of about $100,000 on our present screen sales. This accounts for the $200,000 loss at the end of the "project fails—demand high, competitor's product introduced" series of branches.

The notion of "expected value," already suggested by some of the figures mentioned, is common in decision-tree analyses as well as others. Expected value is a kind of average return. For instance, at the very top of the tree we have a profit figure of $500,000 if demand is high and no competitor comes out with a rival new product. But the chances of that happening are only 20 per cent, in our opinion. If we took this chance over and over for a long period of time, therefore, we would average a $100,000 gain (twice making $500,000 for every eight times we make nothing). The expected value is thus $100,000. Expected values are shown all down through the tree, equaling in each case the gain or loss multiplied by the probability.

The notion of "position value" is also useful. If we authorize the development work, and if it succeeds, we will have the option of going ahead into production or delaying production (second decision stage). Knowing what we do today, we would go ahead, for the four expected values of going ahead are $100,000, $180,-000, $5,000, and 0—a total of $285,000 and considerably more than the expected values of the "delay production" branch. We call this $285,000 the position value of decision #2 because it is the total expected value of the course of action we would in all probability take, knowing what we know now, if we could make decision #2. (Note that four other position values can be deduced: $500,000, $200,000, $350,000, and $140,000, respectively, for the decision #3 squares, each representing what would be the preferable course of action to take. Each of these is multiplied by the appropriate probability to give the expected value figure on the part of the limb preceding the decision box).

What appears to be the best course of action today? If we do not authorize the development work, the total expected value is $120,400 ($61,600 plus $58,800 plus 0 plus 0). But if we do authorize the development, we have a 70 per cent chance of a $285,000 position value, or an expected gain of $199,500. From this we must subtract a 30 per cent chance of a $140,000 loss, or $42,000. Clearly a go-ahead decision is the better course in terms of (a) profit maximization and (b) the income and probability figures used.

In this example, for the sake of simplicity, future gains and losses are not discounted. Discounting could be done if desired, however.

To emphasize a point made earlier in this discussion, *neither this decision tree nor any other tells us what to do.* It simply tells us what is our best *bet* in terms of the gains and losses as we see them *now*. We may not want to take the best bet. There may be other projects we would rather explore, or perhaps we would feel more comfortable with a wait-and-see policy. But whatever we decide, the decision tree has led us through much of the problem in a thorough way. It has led us to make a series of judgments, to be specific in our expectations of gain or loss, to get down to brass tacks about different kinds of risk. Since we have done this rather than try to resolve the problem in a debate of unrefined expectations and judgments—"probably," "maybe," "usually," "but suppose . . ."—we may reach a different and better decision.

Critical Path Method

What about the *operation* of plans and programs? Here, too, quantitative methods have proved useful. For example, few problems have taken more management time and caused more managerial headaches than arranging jobs and activities in the most efficient order in terms of time and costs. This was the problem that Diamond Alkali Company took a major step to solve not long ago. In the words of Warren Dusenbury, sales manager for specialty chemicals:

Past experience indicated that, no matter how well we planned, some key facet of our market introduction was usually snarled up. If production, finished-goods shipments, and literature were on target, our distributor training program would be behind schedule. If our sales training and promotional programs were on schedule, then container delivery or production would be delayed. On occasion, after getting our salesmen and distributors all worked up for the big kickoff, delays in delivery of material or promotional literature allowed them to cool off—end result was half-hearted performance when the full program was ready.[4]

Dusenbury and other managers at Diamond Alkali came up with a remarkable solution to such problems: the critical path method. With the help of this method, a market introduction period that originally looked like seventy-six weeks was reduced to thirty-six weeks; and this was only one of the benefits achieved.

The critical path method, or "CPM" as it is popularly called, had been invented and developed long before Dusenbury's group tried it out. In previous years, however, its main applications had been in construction and engineering. CPM was devised in 1957 by members of DuPont and Remington Rand Univac in order to help management plan, schedule, design, and administer the building of large chemical plants. A related technique—Program Evaluation and Review Technique, or "PERT"—was invented in 1958 by the U.S. Navy's Special Projects Office, the Lockheed Missile System Division, and the management consulting firm of Booz, Allen and Hamilton. PERT became famous for speeding the progress of the Polaris missile program. Almost all companies doing work for the Department of Defense have had to become familiar with PERT since 1960. Other governments, too—Canada, for instance—now require CPM or PERT in some defense work.

The notion of task sequencing, which is the basis of CPM, goes back much farther still—probably hundreds of years. Numerous companies are familiar with it. When, for example, International Minerals and Chemical Corporation builds, with Standard Oil of California, a $60 million plant in India and prescribes the sequence of tasks which various managers must

[4] "Applying Advanced Science to Marketing and Ad Plans," *Printer's Ink*, September 24, 1965.

follow for license procurement, management recruiting, purchasing, manufacturing, promotion, and so forth, it is applying the notion of task sequencing (or network analysis, as it is sometimes called). What is new about CPM is that it provides a visual picture of the critical or most time-consuming activities which must be completed before a deadline can be met. In a masterful explanation of CPM, Rein Peterson uses the following analogy:

A project can be thought of in the terms of the familiar roadmap. Suppose that a bus driver leaves city A to travel to city D, via cities B and C. . . . At C he must wait for another connecting bus from Z to arrive before completing his trip. The time duration of the trip from A to D is therefore dependent on the promptness of arrival of the bus from Z. . . . The trip from A to D is lengthened by exactly the amount of time that the bus from Z is late on arrival. Thus it is *critical* for the bus from Z to be on time, especially if the bus waiting at C must be in D at a certain time to make further connections.

The Critical Path Scheduling techniques are based on the drawing of such a "roadmap" of the project. The roads between cities become jobs to be done. Instead of traveling from A to C, waiting for the bus from Z and then continuing on to D, the project "roadmap" may specify that job A must be completed first, then before continuing on to job D one must wait for the completion of job Z.[5]

A CPM diagram shows all project activities, their relationships to one another, and the duration of time each will take. Each activity shown in the diagram is represented by an arrow. Experienced users of CPM are likely to tell you that about 80 per cent of the gain comes in plotting the arrow sequences. The sequence of critical jobs—that is, the sequence which, if delayed at any point, necessarily causes a delay in the final completion time—is typically shown through the middle of the diagram with an extra heavy or colored line.

From a planning standpoint, CPM is significant because it separates planning from scheduling. Previously, the traditional

[5] "Critical Path Scheduling: A Comprehensive Look," *Business Quarterly,* Summer, 1965, p. 70.

Gantt or bar charts were likely to be used for planning a project. Unlike CPM, they used time as a base; with the designation of an activity, the time when it was to be completed was also set, based on scheduling experience. While such charts were (and are) useful, they made it difficult or impossible to see the inter-relationships of many activities, rearrange sequences in the most efficient manner, and keep on top of what was going on and the effect of delays on over-all project time and costs. Under the CPM method, planning and scheduling are distinct steps. Planning or task sequencing is done first; then detailed time schedules are worked out and distributed for use by supervisors. (Of course, time requirements for activities are often used in the first step to determine the critical paths.)

Another significant thing about CPM, from a planner's standpoint, is that it shows where "trade-offs" may be needed. For example, it may show what jobs should best be "crashed"—that is, speeded up over normal by pumping more than normal man power and funds into them—in order to advance the completion of the whole project by a certain amount of time.

Inevitably, CPM has limitations. If those men making time estimates and planning sequences of jobs do not know the people and conditions in the organization well or do not take full advantage of the help of experts on various jobs down the line, the arrow diagram will not be worth much. CPM is a crutch neither for poor management nor for poor planning. Another problem is that cost accounting systems often do not provide certain information needed by CPM planners. In addition, the arrow diagrams can get terribly complex on large projects, and breaking them down by levels of complexity is not easy. Also, CPM does not tell anyone what is the one best way of laying out a project. Two network planners with skill and experience may produce different diagrams, and one cannot always be "proved" superior to the other.

Nevertheless, by keeping aware of these limitations, managers can minimize their importance while maximizing the potential benefits of the method. And the potential benefits, as Diamond Alkali and other companies have found, are great.

Characteristics

CPM, according to three experts, can be applied to projects consisting of a well-defined collection of jobs or activities that (1) can be started and stopped in a given sequence and (2) must be performed in an orderly sequence.[6] The first requirement eliminates continuous-flow process activities, such as oil refining, where the operations follow one another with no slack times between. The second would eliminate any collection of tasks that can be performed simultaneously or willy-nilly, with none dependent on completion of the other.

Users of CPM may emphasize, when describing their experience with it, how often the first "cut" at a network diagram is revised after review and study. They also emphasize that the amount of detail put into a diagram depends largely on what managers need. The amount of detail is referred to as the "level of indenture." Two supervisors on a project, with different needs and resources, might call for diagrams with different levels of indenture.

Once a CPM diagram has been completed, management may find it desirable to transform parts of it into modified Gantt or bar charts for the use of various supervisors and project managers. Such charts would show the activities which concern a supervisor in their proper relationship to each other, where and how much slack time exists (slack time is the amount of delay that may occur between activities without affecting the completion date), and scheduled completion times in their more familiar deadline form. The reason for this step is that supervisors may have trouble understanding CPM diagrams and need the transla-

[6] F. K. Levy, G. L. Thompson, and J. D. Wiest, "The ABC's of the Critical Path Method," *Harvard Business Review*, September–October, 1963, p. 98.

tion into more conventional control-chart form done for them.

CPM differs from PERT in its use of time estimates. Where CPM uses but one time estimate for a task, PERT uses three: an optimistic estimate, a pessimistic estimate, and a most likely estimate. Where time requirements for jobs are difficult to estimate and it is easier to use a *range* of possibilities, PERT may be preferred. This is likely to be the case with research and development projects in new areas of technology.

Are computers necessary for CPM? Some popular impressions to the contrary, the answer is no. Manual methods work perfectly well for networks involving up to a few hundred activities. The people at Diamond Alkali, in the case referred to, did their network with pencil and paper, and many other management groups have by-passed the computer with similar success. Sometimes they will make the manual computations easier by devising short cuts; for instance, breaking down a large and complicated network into parts and treating each part as a network unto itself. Some precision will be lost this way, but probably not very much in terms of the margin of error taken for granted in time estimates. Where computers come in handy is on cases involving more than a few hundred activities which must be diagramed in one plot and where managers are likely to want to experiment with revisions in the network or in tentative trade-offs. Then in a matter of minutes they can ascertain how a change might affect the whole project. Computer manufacturers have developed ready-made programing systems for CPM users.

Procedures

The first stage of CPM is breaking a project down into discrete jobs or activities. The Diamond Alkali people, for example, broke down their marketing plan into such activities as field sales, advertising, trade shows, preparation of visuals, distributor training, and so forth.

The first breakdown is likely to be in terms of the big jobs;

then these will be divided into the more detailed activities that make them up. For example, the first breakdown may call for preparation of a sales brochure. The next breakdown may divide that job into such subtasks as preparation of rough copy, preparation of graphs, preparation of layout by an agency, revision and approval, final copy and artwork, final approval, and printing.

Then the arrow diagram is prepared. In this stage, managers do not worry about time or cost estimates, but only about what jobs must be done first, what tasks cannot be started until other tasks are completed, what activities can be done at almost any time, and questions of that nature. As already indicated, the first copy of such a network is likely to lead to a series of revisions as managers ponder what is most practical, economical, and efficient under the conditions anticipated.

The next stage is to add time estimates. The figure put on a job should reflect the time normally required to do such a task.

The diagram may show a number of paths leading from the start to the finish. The sequence of jobs requiring the longest time is the critical path. The sum of the times along the critical path equals the time the whole project requires. There can be more than one critical path in a complex network.

In 1964 Minnesota Mining and Manufacturing Company planned a major merchandising campaign with the help of CPM. Management considered the method extremely helpful in planning the project as well as in administering it when the work was under way. The network is shown in Exhibit IV.[7]

Other Methods

Decision trees and CPM are by no means the only quantitative methods which can help the planner in industry, government, education, or the military. There is mathematical programing, which has been used by oil companies. There is simulation, which

[7] Reprinted by permission from *The Business Quarterly*, Summer, 1965, pp. 82–83.

Exhibit IV.
Critical Path Scheduling Diagram
The 3M Company Merchandising Promotion

NOTE: Critical path indicated in bold line. ➡

NOTE: Events 28 and 32 are repeated on the opposite page for convenience of presentation.

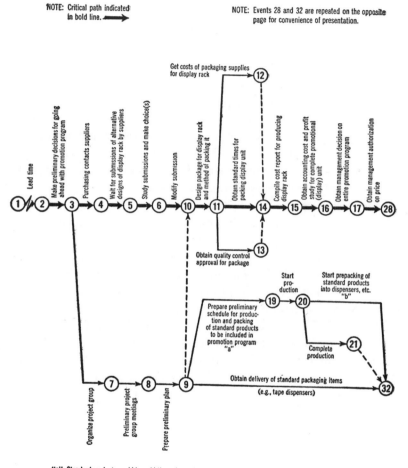

"a" Standard products could be sold through regular channels if final approval (event 16-17) not received.

"b" Some dispensers, etc., always in stock.

From The Business Quarterly, Summer, 1965.

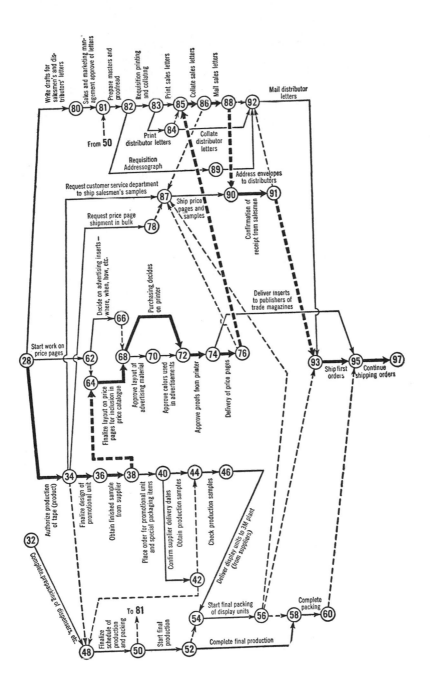

has been used to show how changes and events in one part of a distribution system will likely affect operations in other parts of the system. There is capital budgeting. There is the Bayesian method (often used with decision trees). Methods have been proposed for translating a new product planning and evaluation problem into the many kinds of management judgments which must be made and then in turn expressing these judgments in numerical form so that comparisons can be made and different combinations of judgment experimented with. And still other techniques and approaches have been used or proposed.

Which of these methods will be most useful for a management group, only it can tell. What is important is the strong likelihood that among the available methods there will be one or more which will help managers do a superior job of planning. Some methods can help in the strategic phases—decision trees, for instance. Others can help in the implementational phase—the critical path method, for instance. And some can help in both phases, depending on how they are used. A decision tree might help us to decide *whether* to include a certain kind of product development in our goals. Later, when we begin exploring alternatives of *how* best to go about a given product development project, a decision tree might help us choose between alternative approaches. And there is the ever-present prospect, of course, that simply by using these methods managers will come to fuller understandings with each other and develop better teamwork.

Corporate Transformation

9

Over the years, writers and speakers have cited many virtues of planning. It has allowed more orderly programs of growth through acquisitions, expansion, and research and development. It has made possible greater efficiency in manufacturing and marketing. It has lent itself to management efforts to increase stability of employment. It has stimulated attempts to divide up work more intelligently and coordinate programs more effectively.

The most significant gains from planning, however, have little to do with efficiency, orderliness, or stability. What matters most of all about planning is that it helps and encourages management to put more emphasis on opportunities and initiative. It is a tool for enhancing the *will* of managers, bringing within their grasp a whole new world of possible achievements. Planning makes it possible for organizations to make the great leap from an animal-like form of existence to a higher, more purposeful manner of operation.

The Primitive Organization

Animal-like behavior has characterized so many corporate operations in the past that some future historian may well decide to classify the last two hundred or so years as the age of the primitive corporation—an age of a relatively low order of organizational life and intelligence. If he notes some brilliant exceptions to this blanket characterization, he may call them precursors of the evolution to come.

In what ways has corporate behavior been primitive? For one thing, it has been static rather than dynamic; its movements have tended to be reflex movements rather than planned movements; its philosophy has been one of reacting to events rather than molding them. "Its [the average company's] basic structure," H. Igor Ansoff has said, "is designed to maximize internal efficiency and is hostile to change. . . . In many firms product-market change is viewed as a necessary transient, to be endured but not encouraged."[1] Even in the relatively dynamic aerospace industry, until recently, Ansoff notes that a common attitude was that "nothing is wrong with the firm that a nice long production run couldn't cure."

Paleontologists tell us that many animals became extinct because they did not adapt: the mastodon was too specialized in feet and teeth to survive when geological and climatic conditions changed; Brachiosaurus, the bulkiest of the dinosaurs, was too ungainly to survive when more mobility was required. What of the many companies and industries in the United States and other Western nations which become too specialized to change? If the corporate organization is viewed as a kind of organism, with its departments and divisions taking the place of corporal functions and its supervisors and employees taking the place of cells, surely all of those firms that have thrived on exploiting a market need or economic condition, but lacked the will or foresight to change as the opportunity dried up, can scarcely be ranked much higher than the extinct creature.

Another aspect of primitive behavior in organizations is unwillingness to anticipate the consequences of industrial change

[1] "The Firm of the Future," *Harvard Business Review*, September–October, 1965, p. 170.

and to feel some responsibility for these effects. There are many familiar examples. In the latter part of the nineteenth century, American industrial pioneers took advantage of the corporate form to create huge trusts in the oil, railroad, and other industries. These trusts served an important and immediate purpose, but they also gave their creators monopolistic powers which were soon misused; the tycoons who formed the trusts and combines were unwilling to accept responsibility for these aftereffects, with the result that government had to step in and curb their powers with the antitrust laws. Again, the food and drug industries pioneered with great technological advances which, while essential to a rising standard of living, also led to opportunities for unscrupulous profit seekers; adulteration, misbranding, misleading packaging, and other abuses took place. Industry's unwillingness to anticipate such abuses and take some responsibility for them again made it necessary for Washington to intervene with food and drug laws, truth-in-advertising bills, and other measures.[2]

We admire the pioneers of great organizational and technological changes. But their lack of interest in looking ahead another step to the social consequences is a manifestation of primitive behavior. They were concerned only with the immediate, the visible, the apparent. Whatever the reason—greed, preoccupation, ignorance of an alternative, or conceptual inability—their behavior is not essentially different from that of the predator that so consumes a food supply that the balance of nature is upset and ultimately threatens the predator itself.

Today the corporation is producing new revolutions which will affect society. Television is one such example, bringing to business the means not only to educate and entertain far better than before but also to influence more with advertising. Promotion to young people of cigarette smoking and drinking, for instance, can be more effective on television than in the printed media. Will advertisers and broadcasters feel concerned about the

---

[2] For a fuller discussion of such cases, see Robert W. Austin, "Responsibility for Social Change," *Harvard Business Review*, July–August, 1965, p. 45.

potential impact of their commercials on teen-age society? Already there are signs that some corporate leaders, at least, have adopted a forward look and decided to modify their advertising campaigns appropriately. If effective steps are taken in this direction, they will represent a significant departure from the typical management behavior of the past.

The primitive corporation of today is far more vulnerable than was its predecessor of decades ago. If its prospects for long life and prosperity were questionable then, they are drastically curtailed now. One reason for this is the acceleration of product change and proliferation, so that a company's offerings are threatened not only by competitors within the industry but also by market invasions from companies outside the industry. Companies manufacturing products in more than one industry account today for about two-thirds of all manufacturing sales; and among the largest thousand United States companies, there is a striking increase in the number of firms offering products in a wide variety of product categories. This trend makes corporate life exceedingly precarious for the company which becomes fixed in its ways and oblivious to change. The rapid rise in industrial research and development has a similar effect. About the same as plant and equipment expenditures fifteen years ago, R&D budgets are now over eight times as great as outlays for physical facilities. Not surprisingly, technological forecasting, once regarded as an oddity, has suddenly become a serious business for companies that want to stay in the race.

To make the primitive organization more vulnerable still, the attitudes and values of young people have been changing. The talented young person appears to be particularly dissatisfied with traditional chain-of-command notions, which happen to be most common in the primitive firm. There is increasing evidence that the industry which cannot offer youth challenge at the beginning of a career (not just after years and years of service) will find itself in a vicious cycle, losing talented young people to other employers and the professions and hence forced to become more regimented and less appealing than ever.

In short, we are witnessing upheavals in the environment for corporate life which threaten the existence of business as we have known it in the past. A higher order of management intelligence, once a luxury, is now becoming a condition of survival. An eloquent analogy was made in a recent issue of a company journal:

At exactly 0513, the 18th of April, 1906, a cow was standing at 123° 20′ West longitude, 37° 58′ North latitude—somewhere between the main barn and the milking shed on the old Shafter Ranch in California minding her own business. Suddenly, the earth shook, the skies trembled, and when it was all over, there was nothing showing of the cow above ground but a bit of her tail sticking up.

For the student of change, the Shafter cow is a sort of symbol of our times. She stood quietly enough, thinking such gentle thoughts as cows are likely to have, while huge forces outside her ken built up all around her and—within a minute—discharged it all at once in a great movement that changed the configuration of the earth, and destroyed a city, and swallowed her up.[3]

Moralizing on this event, the writer went on to argue that if business does not "learn to understand and guide the great forces of change at work in our world today, we may find ourselves, like the Shafter cow, swallowed up by vast upheavals in our way of life—quite early some morning."

Of course, the business corporation does not face this situation alone. Much the same dangers confront the primitively managed organization in nearly all fields. In education, government, community service, and the military, no less than in industry, the price of preoccupation with current operations is becoming very high.

Rise of the Purposeful Corporation

The primitive corporation will not become extinct overnight. But it has begun to pass from the economic scene, and it will

3 "The Dynamics of Change," *Kaiser Aluminum News,* Vol. 24, No. 1 (Oakland, Calif.: Kaiser Aluminum and Chemical Corp., 1966).

continue to fade in the future, but more rapidly as time goes on. Taking its place is what might be called the purposeful corporation. A salient feature of the latter is the longer time perspective of its management. This means that it chooses its action today with a view to where it wants to be tomorrow; more important still, management can justify more ambitious, more creative programs because of its time horizons. To a remarkable extent it can make the things happen that it wants to happen. It will not be able to control prices or achieve profit security, so long as there is effective competition, but it will be able to alter marketing, production, and financial conditions.

Thus the purposeful corporation is not a creature of its environment, but a shaper of its environment. Its ability to make things happen through planning stimulates its will to set ambitious goals, and these goals in turn motivate management to increase its planning ability. The purposeful corporation learns there is practically no legitimate business goal that cannot be achieved through planning, if management's desire is strong and there is sufficient time for accomplishment. Just as incredibly complex skills and areas of knowledge can be mastered by an individual if the subject is broken down into small enough segments and the person is given sufficient time for learning, so the corporation can accomplish the seemingly impossible when the steps to the goal are reduced to manageable size through planning and adequate time is allowed. This is one reason that so much attention has been given in this volume to inside-out planning. Tied closely to the corporation's talents, values, and resources, the inside-out approach is geared to what the organization can accomplish without insuperable demands being placed on management for retraining and "buying time" for development work.

On the surface, at least, the difference between the purposeful and the primitive corporation is not dramatic. Both types of organization may have great energy, acumen, resources, shrewdness. Given the same crisis or problem to cope with, each may react in about the same manner. What managers in the purposeful corporation do differently is look ahead more and, during an average day, spend more time on opportunities, less time on operating problems. They engage in the same activities as their counterparts in the primitive organization, but in different proportions. Day by day and month by month, this difference may be scarcely noticeable. But its cumulative impact over time is enormous. (To use the analogy with evolution again, similarly inconspicuous differences have always marked new variations in a species.)

Bearing in mind this lack of dramatic contrast, let us look more closely at the unique powers of the purposeful corporation to *create* markets and opportunities. What kinds of things can it do that are impossible—or, at least, generally impossible—for the primitive company?

For one thing, it can make technological break-throughs, not sporadically or accidentally, but with regularity and high probability of profit. Some purposeful companies today are planning steps and aspects of transportation systems that will require twenty-five to fifty years for development: planes fueled perhaps by liquid hydrogen and flying at hypersonic speeds, intermodal containers for air freight, high-speed trains for cities, advanced hydrofoil and surface-effect ships, and others. Other purposeful companies—ITT and Bell and Howell, for instance—are planning the development of electronic mail systems in which letters are automatically opened and scanned at a sender station, the words converted into electronic impulses and sent over wires, and the letter reproduced and sealed in a receiver station—all in a matter of seconds. One could go on at length with such examples. They are becoming increasingly familiar. And several already shine brilliantly in the historical record, such as AT&T's laying of television wires ("video pairs"), on the recommendation of Bell Laboratories, years before the advent of successful commercial television.

Why can such break-throughs be made only occasionally by the primitive corporation? They require (increasingly, as technology becomes more sophisticated) the taking of many steps, the co-ordination of many "subprograms," the making of investments in a certain order, the involvement of dissimilar disciplines and departments. The electronic postal system, for instance, demands far more than a series of inventions in facsimile transmission. The technical work must be phased in and coordinated with studies of the mail system, legal investigations and arrangements, research in information theory, marketing research, and joint ventures with other organizations. Only the purposeful corporation, working with major plans and hundreds or even thousands of subplans, can hope to produce the sense of commitment and continuity of effort that are essential if the breakthrough is to be achieved.

At present, regular technological break-throughs characterize only a minority of industries, such as aerospace and electronics. But as the concept of the purposeful corporation spreads, we shall see break-throughs occurring far more often in other industries, such as textiles, retailing, housing, publishing, food, and agriculture.

A second type of achievement for the purposeful corporation is progress in very complicated areas where actions and events in a multitude of sectors are highly interdependent—where, in short, the so-called "systems approach" is essential. To illustrate, when International Minerals and Chemical Corporation invests in production facilities for India or the Spanish Sahara, it takes what it calls the "total agriculture" approach. It seeks to relate its ideas for food products to the total agronomy of the country, types of seeds needed, the fertilizers that are necessary, prospective markets for crops, local political considerations, and other factors. It realizes that no matter how good a product, service, or manufacturing facility, the latter can succeed only if it fits successfully into the local pattern of needs and services.

Similarly, Ralston Purina learned to adopt a systems approach in Colombia, South America. Seeing the crying need in Colombia for low-cost meat, milk, and eggs, the company built a feed mill and began educating farmers and dealers. But the feed mill used corn which the local people had been eating, and this upset the local market. Learning from this experience, Ralston Purina employed a broader systems approach when it marketed milo (a grain sorghum). With the cooperation of local Colombian farm officials, it brought in milo seed and guaranteed each grower who used it a cash market for his crop. It set the price of this seed so as not to interfere with local corn production. It improved local storage and transportation facilities. It provided consumer education services for its food products and, where local distribution agencies were inadequate, it did its own retailing of poultry products.[4] All of these activities *together* were important to the success of the venture or of any part of it.

The systems approach can rarely be used by the primitive organization. The reason, of course, is that in both conception and execution the approach demands careful thinking ahead and, in particular, commitments to many kinds of action and sequences of action that are far from obvious at the outset. These actions often mean that the company must *change* conditions and markets so that desired opportunities *will* arise. Clearly, all this calls for a kind of organizational intelligence which is above the primitive level.

In the modern world, with all its interdependencies and complexities, the systems approach is increasingly becoming a "must" for economic and social progress. Although there are magnificent examples of it in the work of some companies and government agencies, it is far from common on the industrial scene. Our primitively managed public and private organizations go on repeating the age-old mistake of building a spectacular new highway, building, machine, or other facility without regard to the way it must fit into the local scene, and so the technical perfec-

---

[4] See Ray A. Goldberg, "Agribusiness for Developing Countries," *Harvard Business Review*, September–October, 1966, pp. 88–89.

tion of the creation goes for little. As this practice changes, with the spread of purposeful corporations, we shall see great improvements in the quality and sophistication of innovation.

The purposeful corporation is capable of still another type of achievement, which is generally beyond the reach of the primitive firm. Its larger organizational "brain" enables it to recognize a whole range of desirable goals which are beyond the comprehension of less advanced companies. Hence we are seeing the beginning of a trend of momentous importance to the corporation and society: companies seizing the initiative in solving social, cultural, educational, and public problems that were traditionally considered to be in the exclusive domain of government. While this trend has not yet gained much momentum, there is unmistakable evidence of its movement: cases like United States Gypsum pioneering in urban renewal, Litton Industries undertaking training programs for the Peace Corps, General Electric drawing up a master plan for national development of the oceans by 1990, DuPont developing training courses for prisoners in federal penitentiaries, Lockheed working out new operating systems for hospitals and medical centers, North American Aviation formulating new patterns of law enforcement for small city police forces, and others. (In 1967 examples of this kind were numerous enough to become the subject of The Chase Manhattan Bank's bulletin, *Action Report*.)

As this trend takes hold, words like "business," "industry," and "management" will acquire new meanings for the public. The image of the corporation will be transfigured; it will acquire glamour because of its versatility in carrying out new ideas and expressing the will of leaders to produce change. It will no longer find it difficult to recruit the most talented young people, and business-government relations will become more constructive.

Planning, as we have seen, is a tool of management, and no more than that. It can be no better than the improvements in decision making which it helps to produce. Further, as a tool, planning is not always unique or exciting; sometimes it consists of fairly dull, routine procedures. The attitude of leading planners and planning-minded organizations, on the other hand, is a different matter. Here are people whose aims and values are intrinsically exciting. They seek to stimulate in their companies and agencies a sense of mission and, through that, a feeling of vitality. "Someone catches the rhythm and it goes all through the organization," Amory Houghton, Jr., of Corning Glass, once said. That is the spirit the planner hopes to generate and regenerate. In business and government at large, he has not been notably successful yet. But he will be, and the world will then become a different place in which to live.

Index

147